THE MOMS ON CALL GUIDE TO BASIC BABY CARE

The First 6 Months

Laura Hunter, LPN, and Jennifer Walker, RN, BSN

Revell

Grand Rapids, Michigan

© 2007 by Laura Hunter and Jennifer Walker

Published by Revell
a division of Baker Publishing Group
P.O. Box 6287, Grand Rapids, MI 49516-6287
www.revellbooks.com

Fifth printing, September 2008

Printed in the United States of America

Library of Congress Cataloging-in-Publication Data
Hunter, Laura (Laura A.), 1971–
    The moms on call guide to basic baby care : the first 6 months / Laura
Hunter, and Jennifer Walker.
        p.   cm.
    ISBN 10: 0-8007-3188-3 (pbk.)
    ISBN 978-0-8007-3188-5 (pbk.)
    1. Infants—Care. 2. Mother and child. I. Walker, Jennifer, 1969– II. Title.
RJ61.M664 2007
618.92′02—dc22   2006033094

Published in association with the literary agency of Mark Sweeney & Associates, Bonita Springs, Florida 34135.

There are so many families that have encouraged and uplifted us along the way. We have been overwhelmed by the generosity and support that has been so freely given.

It is our sincere honor to thank the doctors of North Atlanta Pediatric Associates: Dr. John Knox, Dr. Susan Harrell, Dr. Phil Weiss, Dr. Tama Fuller, and Dr. Elizabeth LeDuc, as well as Rosalind Konter, RNP, and Patty Sullivan, RNP.

We would also like to thank the following families for their specific contributions and enthusiasm:

Kenny and Wanda Rogers
Janet Schultz and Oscar Olin
Shirley Verwers
The Clines
Denise and Dominic Mazzone
Stephen and Lynne Olin
Sharon Box
Tony, Lisa, Donita, Marc, and Cory Walker
Stephanie Birtman
Laura and Patrick Tate
Pamela Ledford-Dyer
The family at the Restoration Church of North Atlanta
The adorable patients of North Atlanta Pediatrics
The Harringtons
The Abrams
Mark and Gwen Brague from MGB design group for putting together the DVD and for hours of laughter

Of course we thank our loving and talented husbands, Jim and Tim. We would have never made it through this without you.

And last but not least, thanks to the eight little darlings that really taught us how to love: Kayla, Allison, Blake, Patrick, Brent, Grayson, Hamilton, and Bryce.

Contents

Mom-to-Mom Testimonials

"It was unbelievable how rested she was the next day. That swaddle really helped her to sleep! She was so calm and happy, like a different baby altogether."

Katherine C.

"Zachary is doing very well. I still can't believe what a miracle worker you are. He sleeps twelve hours a night. What a lifesaver! I just flip through your book for the answers. Plus, I think just showing us that all it really takes is a lot of love and a little discipline has helped guide us."

Karin S.

"We tell your story *all* the time. People just cannot get over the fact that my baby slept through the night every single night when we started your routine! Then, after one night of being out of the swaddle, she slept soundly every single night and slept *late* to top it off. It is just *amazing*. We are so indebted to you. . . . And we love the three-day rule; it gives us hope when something changes in her routine.

We know many parents whose children *still* do not sleep through the night at 18 months! We told your story again at dinner."

Michelle C.

"I wanted to thank you again and I am so thankful that God has blessed you with this special gift. You have given me the confidence I needed to do this with Bailey."

Christine

"Thank you so much again. Jordan is doing great now; your routine worked, and you clued me in to the idea that he may have a GI problem—and he did. Thanks to the routine, Jordan even found his smile this week. Thank you so much!"

Jennifer H.

"I just wanted to let you know that Haley has been sleeping from 10:00 p.m. until 5:00 a.m. almost every night, then she goes back to bed until 7:00 a.m. We are so thankful we were given your name! We will certainly pass it along to *everyone* we know."

Tina & Drew B.

"I can't believe it's been a year since we sought your help with our son Bradley. I'm not sure if I could have made it through this first year without your help. I continue to share my success story with expectant mothers. You are so blessed to have such a gift and I thank God for your help every day."

Jennifer O.

"It is all about becoming educated as a new parent to build that foundation for raising great kids while keeping your home life intact. I plan to use Moms on Call for whatever needs arise."

Liz H.

"Avery has been pretty much sleeping through the night. She sleeps somewhere between 10:00 and 10:30 p.m. and gets up anywhere between 5:00 and 6:00 a.m. There are some days where she wakes up at 4:00 a.m., but these aren't as common. She's such a happy baby, and I'm grateful your tips have helped me to enjoy Avery that much more."

Tina F.

"It is my wish that every expectant parent whom you encounter reads this right away!"

Hope H.

"I think that we were scared to do the 'just let her cry it out' thing, but it really wasn't that bad, and it took just a few nights. Thank you, thank you! Please feel free to use us as an example of parents who were 'parenting by accident' and then followed your instructions and discovered the joy of a system that works."

Beatrice L.

Introduction

We are Laura Hunter, LPN, and Jennifer Walker, RN, BSN, two moms and pediatric nurses who decided it was time to write a how-to child care book that moms could really use—a book by moms and for moms that addresses reality. No psychobabble, no exhaustive list of disorders that could cause immediate anxiety in the calmest of mothers. No, we wanted something different, something we knew moms needed.

How did we know? Well, between us, we are raising eight children: two girls, two sets of twin boys, and two singleton boys. We are doing so with no nannies, no night nurses, no live-in family, and rarely a babysitter. The clincher is what we do to help earn enough money to be home during the day to enjoy each and every sloppy meal and stay home at night to snuggle up to whichever child has the current virus that is going around the school.

As we mentioned, we are pediatric nurses. But we are also nurses on call. When the busy nine-thousand-patient pediatric office we work for is closed and moms have questions after hours, they page us. So from 5:00 p.m. to 8:30 a.m. every weekday and all weekend, the pager goes off. Any worry and need that a mom is experiencing about her child, be it medical or otherwise, we answer. And this is what we have been doing for the past several years.

After about the three hundredth call concerning basic infant care, I (Laura) decided I had to do something to help teach these new moms how to care for their infants. I decided to do infant care consultations. Jennifer and I developed a packet of information and instructions for new parents. Then I went into parents' homes and had a two-hour consultation in which I went over the materials that we developed, including helping parents get their babies to sleep and educating them on common infant care issues. After the first consult, we knew we had found what parents desperately needed. Testimonial after testimonial from pleased parents came pouring in.

Now, the bulk of our clientele was well-read in the art of child care. With each book they read, they hoped to find a secret or a formula that would magically make them amazing and confident parents. As we all know, that did not happen. What did happen was that confused and anxious new parents appeared on our caller ID in search of something better—and they found it. Then they told two friends, and so on it went. So here we are as the result of the popular demand for the real story. Together we developed this need-to-know manual that shares the realities of parenting.

There is a common fear of doing the wrong thing or making the wrong choice. When your baby is born, it is like a new part of your heart blossomed that you never knew was there. This concept is impossible to explain; it can only be felt. We have been there. I (Jennifer) was so nervous with baby number one (Grayson) that it was all I could do to leave him in the care of his incredibly capable and loving grandmother.

We have also felt the sting of leaving baby number one to go to work. That first day is a heartbreaker, and we suffered through it. By the time both sets of twins came along, working outside the home was no longer an option for us. Taking calls from home was a great compromise. Difficult, yes, but it has allowed us to interact with other moms in a way only another mom can, with a heart of compassion and understanding.

We did *not* do everything "right" with our kids. We are learning along the way, just like everyone else. We learned about the reality of parenting. And we too read the popular baby books. We got particularly frustrated when the advice assumed that there was only one child in the household, or that parents have to deal with only one child at a time.

Most of the books left us feeling overwhelmed. It seemed as if they promised some instant fix that never came. If you are looking for a false sense of perfection, you will not find it here. What we hope you will find here is a succinct, easy-to-read reference guide.

Children are amazing and wonderful creatures, full of mystery and wonder. We desire to use our experience and education to help you enjoy the treasure that God has so graciously given you. He thought you were the best parent for your child or children. You may not have a degree or even a good role model, but he chose you. We want to help equip you with some of the information that we know moms need. This book will not make you a perfect parent, but perhaps it can help you enjoy the ride.

This is the condensed, anxiety-free version of proper child care techniques. And in it you will find excerpts of real calls that we've gotten from actual patients (names excluded, of course). Feel free to use the following pages as guidelines for proper baby care. May this journey bless and enrich your life.

When to Seek Medical Care

Anytime that you are concerned about your baby or notice any symptoms, call your pediatrician's office. Sometimes babies have obvious symptoms like a fever, and other times there is just something that you can't explain; call it mother's intuition or a nagging feeling that something may be wrong. Those are both valid reasons to seek medical attention. Many of the instructions in this book vary from pediatrician to pediatrician. When it comes to your child's care, you are responsible for making the final decisions.

This book and DVD are designed to provide information on the care of babies. They are intended as reference material only, not as a medical manual. They are sold with the understanding that neither the author nor the publisher are engaged in rendering medical, health, or any other kind of personal professional services in the book. The reader should consult the services of a competent pediatrician, registered dietician, or other medical professional. The author and publisher specifically disclaim all responsibility for any liability, loss, or risk—personal or otherwise—to any parent, person, or entity with respect to any illness, disability, injury, loss, or damage to be caused, or alleged to be caused, directly or indirectly, by the use or application of any of the contents of this book.

The book and DVD should be used only as a supplement to your pediatrician's advice, not as a substitute for it. It is not the purpose of this book and DVD to replace the regular care of, or contradict the advice from, the American Academy of Pediatrics, or any pediatrician, nutritionist, registered dietician, or other professional person or organization. This text should be used only as a general guide and should not be considered an ultimate source of child care, child feeding, food preparation and storage, or any other information. You are urged to read other available information and learn as much as possible about child care and the nutrition and feeding of young children. Mention of specific companies, organizations, or authorities in this book does not imply endorsement by the publisher, nor does their mention imply that they endorse this book.

Every reasonable effort has been made to make this book and DVD as complete and as accurate as possible. However, there may be mistakes, both typographical and in content. Therefore, this text should be used only as a general guide. You should discuss with your pediatrician the information contained in this book before applying it. This book and DVD contain information only up to the copyright date. New information, or information contradicting that which is found in this book, should be actively sought from your child's competent medical professionals.

How to Use the DVD

There was once a time when mothers taught their daughters the ins and outs of child care. In this day and age, with medical research evolving so fast and the family unit dispersed both far and wide, it is rare to find a family that is able to get all of their questions answered in that manner. That is where we come in. We have created the DVD included in this book to help show you how to perform some basic infant care tasks. Those we selected are ones that are hard to explain with the written word and more easily learned through demonstration. What a concept—your own personal pediatric nurse to demonstrate how to do the complicated stuff! The skills that are essential to the success of a good night's sleep and more are as follows:

- Diapering
- Massaging tear ducts
- Taking a rectal temperature
- Nail clipping

- Nasal suctioning
- Bath time routine
- Swaddling*
- Bedtime routine
- The three-day rule

You will get so much more out of these materials if you watch the DVD and follow along in this book. Enjoy!

*The swaddling techniques that are so essential for infants use a special-size blanket made of a flannel material that stretches in only one direction. These blankets are available at www.momsoncall.com. The dimensions of this blanket are 44 x 44 inches. If you know someone who has a sewing machine that has surging capabilities, you may make extras yourself. The standard-size flannel blanket that is sold in stores will not provide an effective, tight swaddle in the fashion we are showing you. We have also found that other swaddling techniques do not hold as well as what we have developed. It is crucial to swaddle correctly.

THE BASICS

*What Every Mom Needs to Know
about Basic Baby Care*

General Shopping List

Moms on Call recommends having the following items on hand prior to needing them. This will cut down on any middle-of-the-night trips to the pharmacy after you speak to the pediatrician's office.

We have these items in our own closets and diaper bags. So if you want to know what two pediatric nurses with eight kids keep handy, read on!

- Infant Tylenol (1 bottle) and Children's Tylenol Suspension (2–3 bottles)
- Fever-All suppositories (acetaminophen, the same ingredient for fever reduction found in Tylenol but in suppository form)
- Benadryl Liquid (2–3 bottles)
- Normal saline nose drops (Little Noses is our favorite; get the plain drops.)
- Vitamin A&D Ointment

Note:
Do not administer any medications to your baby without consulting your pediatrician.

21

- √ Vaseline
- Lotrimin AF (may be found in the foot-care section of the pharmacy)
- ✓ Diaper rash cream (Palmer's is one without zinc oxide. You can find it at Babies "R" Us.)
- ✓ Aquaphor Healing Ointment
- ✓ Regular kitchen corn starch
- Aveeno Oatmeal Bath Packets
- Eucerin or Lubriderm lotion
- Cortaid hydrocortisone cream
- Hydrogen peroxide (2–3 smaller bottles)
- Polysporin Antibiotic Ointment
- ✓ Antibacterial hand wash
- 4 x 4 gauze individually packed (2–3 boxes)
- 2 x 2 gauze individually packed (2–3 boxes)
- Band-Aids
- Squeezable ice packs
- Tweezers—diagonal head (2–3)
- Glycerin suppositories
- Baby pear or white grape juice
- Isomil DF (antidiarrhea formula)
- Pedialyte (electrolyte replenisher)
- Canned peaches in heavy syrup
- BD digital thermometer (2–3)
- K-Y Jelly
- Medicine dosage syringes
- Infant gas drops

Note:
Remember to always keep a digital thermometer, a bottle of Infant Tylenol, and a bottle of Children's Benadryl secured in your diaper bag.

- Bug repellent (Skintastic is one particular brand. Spray on hands, then apply to infant sparingly, or just put repellent on baby's clothes and socks.)
- Sunscreen (Water Babies or Spectra by Coppertone are our favorites.)
- Nail clippers by Safety First (with the white hand-grip)
- Long-handled infant spoons (usually one piece of plastic)
- Biz laundry soap (This is great for stain removal—especially if items are soaked overnight, then washed in a regular laundry cycle.)

Bathing

CALL "I have a 1-week-old and I wasn't sure if I could bathe her in her little bath now, or if I should wait until the umbilical cord falls off."

This is a frequently asked question. Your baby likely will have his or her first bath at home. It is unbelievably fun and adorable, but be careful—wet babies are slippery! Support the baby's head until the baby can do so on his or her own.

- Until the umbilical cord falls off, give a sponge bath with no soap and with tepid water (slightly warmer than room temperature).
- After the umbilical cord falls off, regular baths may be given. (Baby soap is optional, but it sure makes them smell good!)

Always make sure that all supplies are kept within arm's reach. A basket is an easy way to ensure that everything is kept together.

You may use an infant bathtub or hold the baby carefully in the regular tub (see DVD). Use non-skid mats and always be cautious to support the baby's head and neck.

We have found that the water in the baby bathtubs gets cold faster than in the adult bathtub.

Fill the adult bath with only one or two inches of water. Never leave your baby in the tub or around water unattended.

Things to have at arm's reach in the bathroom:

- Towels
- Washcloths
- Baby soap
- Soft baby brush

Note:
The DVD demonstration of bathing techniques will be quite helpful.

Bathing every day is fine, but during the first few months, two or three times a week is enough for a full bath. Always rinse your baby well. Babies associate bath time with bedtime. At the very least, sponge the baby down as a nighttime routine.

Females

Do not wash the genital areas with soap. Instead, you can rinse with plain water. Spread the labia (liplike parts) and clean with a diaper wipe or washcloth when taking the diaper off *prior to* the bath.

Males (Circumcised)

After the circumcision is healed, gently pull the foreskin back so the lip of the penis is seen all the way around, and clean well. Do this when you remove the diaper prior to the bath.

Males (Uncircumcised)

Clean the foreskin well. There is no need to retract the skin during the baby's first year. Speak with your doctor for specific care.

Shampooing Hair

Apply a pea-sized amount of baby shampoo to the baby's hair. Scrub the scalp with a soft infant brush. If you are concerned about hurting the soft spot, just scrub gently. Rinse hair well.

Umbilical Cord Care

Keep the umbilical cord dry. Lift up and apply rubbing alcohol with a Q-tip around the base of the cord. Do this at least two or three times a day until it falls off. You may want to cut out a wedge in the diaper so the cord is not covered.

WHEN TO SEEK MEDICAL CARE

- Strong, foul odor

- Oozing yellow/whitish discharge

- Bleeding that runs out of the belly button (more than one teaspoon of bright red blood). Dried blood is okay. The blood that is in the cord is generally leftover maternal blood, not the baby's blood. If the cord has bright red or even persistent dried blood, the pediatrician can usually fix it by putting on a special compound that is painless for the baby.

Bowel Movements

Can you believe how we obsess over our baby's bowel movements? Color, consistency, frequency, and amount of apparent straining are common concerns for moms. Let us set your mind at ease. There is a wide range of what is considered normal for a bowel movement.

After the first week of life, if you are lucky, bowel movements slow down from every feeding to maybe once or twice a day. Once the baby begins to have baby foods or finger foods, they may slow down to one bowel movement a day or even one a week! (If you are not lucky, your twins each have simultaneous and copious stools eight times a day until they are three years old. That's sixteen poopy diapers per day!)

Color

- Breast-fed: generally yellow and seedy; can vary from yellowish brown to green

- Formula-fed: darker in color; can vary from yellow to brown to green

WHEN TO SEEK MEDICAL CARE

- More than one teaspoon of bright red blood at any time

- Less than one teaspoon of bright red blood for three or more stools

- Black tarry stools

- What looks like coffee grounds

- A clay-colored (gray or beige) stool for more than two weeks

Note:
The color of stools will vary from feeding to feeding, generally according to what the baby's body is absorbing and excreting.

Frequency

Depending on whether you breast-feed or formula-feed, the frequency may vary greatly. Early on, the baby may be stooling every feeding, from small amounts to full diapers. However, by the time your baby reaches 6 months old, he or she may stool as frequently as every feeding or as infrequently as once a week. What a difference!

Constipation

True constipation is a term used to describe hard, pebble-like stools. There is a difference between constipation and infrequent stooling. (Infrequent stoolers are gassy and have a large, soft bowel movement every three to seven days.)

Signs of Constipation

- Painful passage of stools when the stool itself is hard and pebblelike
- Abdomen is distended but remains relatively soft
- Decreased appetite

Relief Measures

- You may stimulate a bowel movement with a rectal thermometer or Q-tip with Vaseline or K-Y Jelly. Insert one-fourth of an inch into the rectum and rotate a few times.
- You may give one to two ounces of baby pear or white grape juice every morning until stools are softer.
- Glycerin suppositories are available over the counter (OTC). They are made of sugar water and do not have any medications in them. They just stimulate the bowels to move.
- Babies more than 4 months old may have strained baby food with baby cereals, such as apricots, prunes, peaches, pears, plums, beans, peas, or spinach, at least two times per day. Avoid carrots, squash, and bananas.

Note:
Remember, babies commonly grunt, push, strain, draw up their legs, and turn red when passing a stool. This is normal. Think about what you would do if you had to have a bowel movement while lying down. After the second month or so, many babies pass normal, large, soft bowel movements at infrequent intervals, up to one every seven days. This is generally not abnormal as long as the stool is not hard and does not seem painful for the baby to pass.

WHEN TO SEEK MEDICAL CARE

- No relief after trying the above measures

- Abdominal tenderness when pressing on either side of the abdomen at the level of the belly button

- If fever is present (ask your pediatrician for a fever handout)

- Happens frequently

- Persistent vomiting (see vomiting section)

Note:
Infrequent stooling is not a problem and does not **have** to be treated. It is perfectly normal for many babies and toddlers.

Infrequent Stoolers

Signs

- Soft stools can be every other day to once every seven days.
- Babies may have increased gas and/or fussiness.

Relief Measures

(Use relief measures only if the baby seems uncomfortable and with the approval of your pediatrician.)

- Increase fluids (breast milk or formula) or add one or two ounces of water per day.
- Use Mylicon gas drops.
- You may use rectal stimulation with a rectal thermometer or glycerin suppository as frequently as every other day, with the approval of your pediatrician. If you have to use these for longer than two weeks, consult your pediatrician.

Eye Drainage

CALL "My 2-month-old has watery eyes, and the eyes look a little irritated. Does she have pink eye?"

There are many reasons why a baby may experience eye discharge. Generally, eye drainage is not an emergency. However, it is best to contact your pediatrician if there are any related symptoms such as the ones described below.

Watery eyes or discharge that is clear to yellow in color may come and go until 6 months of age. Your pediatrician may diagnose a blocked tear duct. It is very common.

Care: Wash your hands! Clean the baby's face with a warm (not hot) washcloth and then, using your pinky finger, massage (where the eye meets the bridge of the nose) in a circular motion while applying pressure (see DVD). *Do not apply direct pressure to the eye itself.*

WHEN TO SEEK MEDICAL CARE

- Thick yellow or green discharge that reappears after wiping it away several times a day

31

- No improvement of symptoms after tear duct massage and warm compress three to four times per day for three days (see DVD)

- Eye redness or swelling (especially swelling that goes up to the eyebrow or below the eye approximately one inch or lower)

- Symptoms appeared immediately after a possible foreign body entered the eye. (The sandbox is a great place to get a scratched cornea.)

- Fever (ask your pediatrician for a fever handout). Seek immediate medical attention for a baby less than 3 months old with a rectal temperature of 100.4 degrees or higher.

Viral Discharge

Signs

- Eye redness on the inner lids and/or white part of eye (sclera)
- Watery discharge or thick mucus discharge from eyes (usually occurs with a cold and can produce crustiness in the morning)

Treatment

- Wipe away any mucus with a warm (not hot) washcloth while eyes are closed.
- Treat cold symptoms with OTC decongestant if the baby is more than 3 months old and over 14 pounds.

- After the baby is asleep, apply a thin layer of Vaseline over the eyelashes. This will make it easier to wipe the crustiness off in the morning.

WHEN TO SEEK MEDICAL CARE

- No improvement of symptoms in two or three days

- Eye redness or swelling, especially swelling that goes up to the eyebrow or below the eye approximately one inch or lower

- Fever

- Ear pain

- Sensitivity to light

Bacterial Discharge

Signs

- Yellow-green discharge from eyes that has to be wiped away every twenty to thirty minutes
- Usually will have pinkness or redness to white part of the eye (sclera)
- Puffiness to eyelids (may or may not be present)
- Crustiness in the morning, but mucus recurs every twenty to thirty minutes, even when awake

Treatment

- Antibiotic eye drops (have to be prescribed by the pediatrician)

33

- Warm compresses with a clean, warm (not hot) washcloth
- Treat cold symptoms
- After the baby is asleep, apply a thin layer of Vaseline over the eyelashes to make it easier to wipe the crustiness off in the morning.

WHEN TO SEEK MEDICAL CARE

- No improvement in symptoms after using antibiotic drops for two days

- Showing signs of an ear infection (see p. 65)

- Fever

- Swelling of the eyelids that goes up to the eyebrow or below the eye approximately one inch or lower

Allergy-Related Discharge

Signs

- Itchy eyes with frequent rubbing
- Increased tearing (clear and watery)
- Pinkness or redness to the white part of the eye (sclera)
- No pain or fever
- Seems to occur around the same season or around the same allergen (dog, cat, outdoor play area, etc.)

Treatment

- Benadryl or OTC antihistamine by mouth if approved by your pediatrician
- OTC allergy eye drops (if recommended by your pediatrician according to child's age)

Note:
Always remember to wash your hands frequently.

WHEN TO SEEK MEDICAL CARE

- No improvement of symptoms in two or three days
- Swelling that goes up to the eyebrow or below the eye approximately one inch or lower
- Fever
- Ear pain
- Extreme sensitivity to light

Nail Clipping

CALL "I can't get my baby's fingernails clipped. She keeps moving around so much."

Trim nails after a bath, when the nails are soft. This may take two people at first. You may also try to do this when the child is asleep. Watch the DVD for a nail-clipping demonstration.

Note:
Use nail clippers that have a white handgrip, which are easier for you to hold.

- Trim the toenails straight across to prevent ingrown toenails. You will not need to cut the toenails as often as the fingernails.
- When cutting the fingernails, round off the corners to minimize the chance of your infant scratching himself or herself.
- As the child reaches 12 to 18 months, begin to "name" the different fingers. Children like this game. As they begin to talk, ask them to name each finger as you are clipping them. (The sillier the names, the better!)

Skin Care

You seldom see a child with perfect skin. Baby acne tends to break out the night before you have baby pictures scheduled. Expect skin rashes. Here is a description of some common rashes that are seen in infants.

Baby Acne

These are small, red bumps on the face, chest, scalp, and back. It looks like adult acne, just smaller. It usually begins at 2 to 4 weeks and can last until 4 to 6 months.

- Clean with mild soap and water; there's no need to apply lotions or baby oils.
- This rash can come and go for several weeks.

Drool Rash

This is a splotchy pink area on the chin or cheeks that comes and goes. It can be caused by spitting up, pacifiers that hold drool against skin, or frequent drooling.

• Rinse the baby's face with water after feedings.
• Apply Vaseline to area to protect skin from irritation.

Heat Rash

This consists of prickly pink bumps and splotchy areas. This rash can be seen on skin that touches the mother's skin during breast-feeding or along the back where the baby sweats in the car seat. It likes to pop up where there is moisture and friction.

• Change your baby's position during feedings to change the areas where the baby's skin touches your skin.
• Apply cornstarch powder (not baby powder) to the baby's back or chest. Put the powder in your hand first, and then apply to the affected areas. Be careful not to get the powder or the dispenser anywhere near the baby's face, as infants can choke on the powder.

Moist Areas

These are under the neck, in skin folds. You may use cornstarch to help with moisture. See above.

Dry, Flaky Skin

You may use Eucerin or Lubriderm to moisturize skin. Dry patches may occur behind the knees and elbows, although it may also appear in other areas such as cheeks, diaper area, or face.

- Apply 1 percent hydrocortisone cream minimally twice a day as long as your pediatrician recommends it.
- If the dryness does not clear up in three days or gets worse at any time, call your pediatrician.

Cradle Cap

These are oily yellow scales on the scalp. They begin in the first few weeks of life and can last up to several weeks.

- To help prevent cradle cap, shampoo hair with soap and scrub the scalp with a soft infant brush. Rinse well.
- If cradle cap is already present, wash hair with Neutrogena T-gel if approved by your pediatrician. (Remember to keep it out of the baby's eyes.) Apply to hair and scrub lightly with an infant hairbrush during a bath. Rinse thoroughly. Do this three times a week. Once the rash has cleared, use mild infant soap for shampooing. Do not use T-gel for more than two weeks. If symptoms last longer than two weeks or worsen with treatment, take the baby to the pediatrician.

- If severe crustiness occurs, put some baby oil on the scalp one hour before washing to soften the crust. Make sure to rinse well.

Diaper Rash

- **Redness.** Minimize use of diaper wipes; instead, use a wet washcloth or soft paper towels. Leave the diaper area open to air (for as long as is practical). Change diapers frequently. Use diaper cream (Vitamin A&D, Aquaphor, Gerber, Palmer's, Desitin), and use kitchen cornstarch to keep moisture from irritating the skin.
- **Red and bumpy.** Minimize use of diaper wipes. Leave open to air (again, for as long as is practical). Change diapers frequently. Apply Lotrimin AF three times a day if approved by your pediatrician, and follow with any diaper cream listed above and kitchen cornstarch. Use Lotrimin AF for seven days. If there is bleeding or no improvement in three to four days, see your pediatrician.

Tip: I (Laura) like to use a combination of Aquaphor and Palmer's mixed together, then apply cornstarch. We also recommend Kirkland Diaper Wipes (at Costco), which is the only brand of diaper wipe we recommend using if the baby has a diaper rash. They do not leave any residue and are gentle on the skin. You can also buy these in bulk—a good idea because you will use more than you think.

Teething and Oral Care

CALL "My baby is so fussy. I am wondering if she is teething or has an ear infection."

There is no way to definitively tell whether or not your baby has an ear infection unless the doctor looks in the ear. This can make moms so frustrated!

Teething can begin as early as 2 to 3 months old or as late as 1 year old. My (Jennifer) children had no teeth until they were about 11 months old. They discovered the joy of gumming everything from Cheerios to cheese!

Some children do not have any pain while teething. We all hope for that kind of child!

Teething

Signs

- Increased drooling
- Chewing constantly
- Swollen, red gums

Usually the teeth break through in the following order:

- 2 lower incisors
- 4 upper incisors
- 2 lower incisors and all 4 first molars
- 4 canines
- 4 second molars

Relief Measures

- Massage swollen gums.
- Wet an infant washcloth slightly and put it in the freezer for ten minutes. Allow the baby to chew on it as needed—supervised, of course.
- Give Tylenol as needed for mild discomfort if the baby is older than 3 months and if approved by pediatrician. Try to keep this method of pain control to a minimum.

Note:
It is very difficult to tell the difference between teething and ear pain. If the baby is running a fever for more than two or three days, is not sleeping well, is grabbing at his or her ears, and/or has cold symptoms, call your pediatrician.

Oral Care

- Begin brushing teeth and gums with wet gauze or a wet washcloth wrapped around your index finger. Be careful not to let the gauze slip off your finger.
- Never allow your child to go to sleep with milk or formula residue on his or her gums and teeth. This causes painful tooth decay. That means no bottles in the crib!

- You may use *toddler* toothpaste as soon as the teeth erupt, even though the baby can't spit it out until much later. (Make sure it is fluoride free.)
- When you begin using toothpaste, use only a pea-sized amount.
- Use toothpaste intended for infants/toddlers that can be swallowed.
- You need to help your child brush his or her teeth until around 6 years old.
- Begin flossing when the molars start to touch each other.

The baby's first visit to the dentist should be at around 2 or 3 years old, but it can be earlier if there is noticeable tooth decay or problems, including chipped teeth. We recommend pediatric dentists because they know how to deal with the unique problems that can arise for kids. Be aware that most pediatric dentists will have you sit in the waiting room while your child is treated. Your child will tolerate procedures much better without you (trust us!). Moms often are so anxious that it is difficult to calm the child.

Thrush

This consists of white, irregular-shaped patches that coat the inside of the mouth and sometimes the tongue. Thrush is generally found on the inside of the cheeks and the inside of the bottom lip. (If it is *only* on the tongue, it may not be thrush). The coating cannot be wiped off with your fingernail. Thrush may cause mild discomfort when eating. Call the pediatrician's office if you suspect thrush.

- Nystatin oral suspension can usually be called into the pharmacy if your doctor suspects thrush.
- Boil all bottle nipples and pacifiers every night for five minutes. Also wipe down baby toys that come in contact with the mouth with a germicidal cloth and rinse thoroughly. Do this for the first three days of treatment.
- If breast-feeding, apply Nystatin to irritated areas of nipples with your ob-gyn's approval. Also clean your nipples with vinegar washes (one part vinegar to two parts water) after every feeding and let air dry.

WHEN TO SEEK MEDICAL CARE

- There is no improvement after using Nystatin for seven days.

- The thrush gets worse instead of better.

- Discomfort continues after doing treatment for three to four days.

Twins

CALL "My twins are 4½ months old and still do not sleep at night. We are exhausted!"

Here are the survival tactics that helped us.

1. **When one baby eats, the other does also.** Even if one twin does not appear hungry, feed that one anyway. Keep them on the exact same schedule! It is okay to put them both in bouncy seats and feed them simultaneously with bottles. Just remember to talk softly to both of them and give them each a few minutes of your full attention. Breast-feeders can hold both babies in the football hold (see p. 83) and feed at the same time.

I (Jennifer) did not like the way simultaneous breast-feeding felt and decided to breast-feed one baby and bottle feed the other on an alternating basis. At each feeding, whoever bottle-fed last time became the breast-feeder, and the other one got the bottle. I would breast-feed one baby in the cradle hold (see p. 83) while holding a bottle in the other baby's mouth with my "free" hand. The baby with the bottle was generally propped up on a nearby bouncy seat or Boppy pillow. This way they both were getting at least half of their nutrition from breast milk every day. And they were fed, burped, and changed in forty-five minutes!

It is also good to allow Dad to feed the babies sometimes, whether that's in the middle of the night or one feeding during the day while you nap. He can feed with formula or with pumped breast milk from a bottle. It gives Dad a chance to have that much-needed interaction. It can also give you a chance to get some extra sleep. When you are breast-feeding twins, your body requires as much sleep as possible to continue to produce enough breast milk.

2. **When one baby sleeps, the other does also. Naptimes and bedtimes are the same.** (See point 4 for specific guide-lines for bedtime.) Again, one baby may not seem sleepy at the same time as the other. This is survival mode. They will learn to be on the same schedule, which is part of learning to live in a family environment. One twin may have to learn to sleep more to accommodate the family schedule.

Some parents like to stagger the naptimes so they have an hour to spend with one baby at a time. Once the babies are 4 or 5 months old, this is fine. The feeding and changing schedules prior to that time are entirely too time-consuming (unless you have helpers, such as a night nurse, nanny, or live-in family member).

3. **Use your helpers.** You will be absolutely exhausted in the first two or three years (honestly). If grandma comes for a visit one day, allow her to watch the babies while you nap for an hour or two. If neighbors or friends ask how they can help, allow them to make a meal or arrange for household chores. Many people would love to help if they just had a tangible thing to do. Let others make meals for you. If someone you trust offers to baby-sit, say, "That

sounds great; when are you available?" Think of it this way: the more you allow others to help, the more time you will have to actually enjoy your twins!

4. Use the Moms on Call method of getting your babies to sleep (see p. 99). As early as 5 weeks old, your babies can be bathed, fed, and sleeping five to nine hours per night. This will make the hectic days so much easier. We do realize that some moms do not have the extra hands around at night. Also, single parents of twins are more likely to have to do the bath time and bedtime routines alone. Here is a way to do those routines by yourself.

Put both babies in bouncy seats in the bathroom. Give them a bath, one at a time. While one takes a bath, the other waits in the bouncy seat and may cry or fuss. Once they are both bathed and both sitting in their towels in the bouncy seats, take them one at a time (bouncy seat and all) to get dressed in the nursery. Remember not to leave a baby in the tub unattended for any amount of time. Put the first baby dressed in the bouncy seat momentarily while you dress the other baby. When they are both dressed and back in the bouncy seats in the nursery, play soft music. Feed them their last nighttime feeding (don't forget to burp them). Swaddle them tightly if they're less than 3 months old. Place them in the crib, turn on the white noise, and turn off the lights.

The babies can sleep in the same crib or separate cribs. They can each have a room of their own if you have the space. Take your cues from them. Letting them "cry it out" takes on new meaning with multiples. However, we have often found that one twin can awaken and scream while the other sleeps as if nothing is happening, so do not immediately assume that the crying child will wake the sleeping child. When you have a firm nighttime routine, even if the sleeping child awakens, they can both learn to soothe themselves back to sleep if given three nights of consistency. I know that you do not want the "good sleeper" to have to suffer, but his or her help is needed in teaching the other twin that screaming does not get you an automatic "get out of crib free" card. Three nights, three nights, three nights (see p. 111). It works!

5. **Remember, it gets easier as they get older.** Twins are incredibly labor intensive for the first three years. Double the work, but double the love! The great news is that they will hit a period of time when they are continuous playmates. It is easier to have two 18-month-olds because you are not their only source of entertainment. They will play together and keep each other amused for years. It is wonderful. My (Jennifer) mom is a twin, and she described it this way: "Having a twin is not like having another brother or sister; it's like having another you."

COMMON ILLNESSES

*A Quick Reference Guide
to Disease Processes Common
for This Age Group*

Overview

CALL "My 4-month-old has a frequent cough and a fever."

We frequently get calls regarding common childhood ill-nesses. Here are some general descriptions of illnesses that are usually seen between 0 and 6 months. The following pages are for reference only and are not to be used for diagnostic purposes. Only qualified medical professionals are able to accurately diagnose and treat an illness.

These are the concerns that will be described in the following pages:

- Fever
- Common colds
- Falls
- Lacerations
- Otitis media (ear infections)
- Vomiting
- Diarrhea
- Reactive airway disease/bronchitis/bronchiolitis
- Infant nasal congestion

We also wanted to share with you a list of general symptoms that require immediate medical care. This list includes but may not be limited to the following:

- Seizure activity
- Unresponsiveness
- *Inconsolable* crying for two or more hours
- Abdominal pain that hurts worse if you press one inch to the right or left of the belly button
- A bright red or purple prickly rash that does not blanch to white when you apply pressure with your finger. This rash is noticeable and sometimes looks almost like freckles. In a child who is lethargic and has a fever, this is one sign of meningitis. Other signs include headache, neck stiffness, and lethargy.
- A sudden onset of a hivelike rash all over with facial swelling around the lips and eyes
- Any difficulty breathing. If you are concerned that your child is unable to get air into his or her lungs, go immediately to the emergency room.

Difficulty breathing can be accompanied by the following symptoms:

- Ribs becoming pronounced on inhalations
- Squeaky noise on exhalations
- Breathing faster than sixty times per minute (count how many times the chest rises in one full minute)
- Coarse noise when inhaling (stridor) that sounds like a gasp or squeak with each breath
- Lips are blue or purple
- Cannot stop coughing long enough to breathe

Fever

CALL "My 1-month-old has a fever of 101 rectally."

This is one piece of information that often gets overlooked. Parents need to seek *immediate* medical attention for a baby *less than* 3 months old with a rectal temperature of 100.4 or higher. Babies less than 3 months old have trouble fighting off infection and are more susceptible to illnesses like meningitis. Therefore, we do not tolerate a fever at or above 100.4 rectally in this age group. Amazingly, after the baby turns 3 months old, fevers are not as much of a concern by far and can actually be quite beneficial. Be sure to ask your pediatrician for a fever handout so you'll know what to look for.

We get so many calls about fevers. This is a misunderstood symptom. God designed our bodies to fight off infection. One way the body does that is to turn up the heat when a virus or bacteria is detected, hoping the bacteria or virus will not want to stick around if it gets too hot. Mild fevers in babies *more than* 3 months old can help them to fight off infection.

It is also imperative that you are able to take an accurate temperature (especially if you are trying to decide whether to go to the ER with a newborn). When taking the baby's temperature, we recommend taking rectal temperatures exclusively until the baby is more than 18 months old. A rectal temperature is the most accurate way to take a temperature. The ear, forehead, and pacifier thermometers are just not as accurate in infants. We recommend using a BD Digital Thermometer.

In babies *more than* 3 months old, normal rectal temperatures are between 97 and 100.5 degrees Fahrenheit; we would not consider their temperature to be a fever unless it was over 101 rectally. Temperatures may vary according to several factors, including activity level and time of day.

Taking a Rectal Temperature (See DVD)

1. Lubricate the thermometer with a pea-sized amount of Vaseline or K-Y Jelly.
2. Lay the infant on his or her back as if changing a diaper.
3. Lift the legs so that the rectum is easily seen.
4. Press the on button on the thermometer.
5. Insert the thermometer into the rectum about one-fourth inch or until you can no longer see the silver tip of the thermometer.
6. Hold the thermometer in place for three minutes or until it beeps. (Some models of rectal thermometers will beep only once; the BD brand beeps three times fast.)
7. Remove and read the thermometer.

Treatment

Daytime Treatment

- Seek immediate medical attention for a baby less than 3 months old with a rectal temperature of 100.4 or higher.
- For a baby 3 to 6 months old with a temperature of over 101.5 rectally, call the pediatrician.
- Give extra fluids.
- Fevers generally subside during the day and spike in the late afternoon. There is no need to treat a fever at or under 101.5 rectally unless the child is uncomfortable.

Nighttime Treatment for Babies More Than 3 Months Old

- Put the child to bed wearing cool cotton clothing (no fleece zip-ups or warm blankets). Temperature of the home should be between 68 and 72 degrees.
- If the baby wakes up and feels very hot, undress him or her down to the diaper and give Tylenol, unless Tylenol was given in the last four hours. *Do not take the temperature for ten minutes.* The temperature will spike right when the child awakens. If you give the child about ten minutes of being undressed, the fever will generally come down one or two degrees all on its own. This helps us to avoid a big parental breakdown over a 104.5 rectal temp.
- There is normally a wait at the ER, and by the time you have given the baby fever-control medicine and arrived at the ER, the fever may be under control. However, high fevers may need to be evaluated if they

are accompanied by other symptoms such as

- neck stiffness;
- bright red or purple rash that does not blanch or lighten with pressure;
- persistent vomiting (more than twice);
- severe abdominal pain with pressure;
- inconsolable crying longer than one hour;
- difficulty breathing (not faster breathing; respirations will get faster when there is a fever);
- seizure activity (violent shaking).

WHEN TO SEEK MEDICAL CARE

- For a baby less than 3 months old with a rectal temperature 100.4 or higher

- For a baby 3 to 6 months old with a temperature of over 101.5 rectally, call the pediatrician.

- For a baby with any temperature who is lethargic (like a wet noodle) all day. Not having at least twenty- to thirty-minute periods of playfulness at any temperature can be a sign of illness.

- Fever accompanied by other symptoms such as, but not limited to, a rash, vomiting, decreased movement of a limb, difficulty breathing, inconsolable crying longer than an hour, or an abdomen that is hard like a table when the baby is at rest

Note:

Tylenol does not cure the cause of the fever. It is for comfort only. Once the medication wears off, the fever will come back until the child is no longer sick. Often the child's temperature will not come all the way back down to normal, even with fever-control medicine. It can hover between 101 to 102 degrees rectally in an infant more than 3 months old, even with fever-control medicine. It is also important to note that ibuprofen products such as Motrin or Advil are *not* approved for use in babies less than 6 months of age.

Febrile Seizures

These are generally harmless and are a result of the fever going up too fast, not the fever getting too high. These may last one to three minutes. Usually febrile seizures begin at 6 months to 2 years old, with the first seizure occurring by the time the child is 2 years old. They normally stop by the time the child is 5 to 6 years old. Febrile seizures generally will occur in the first twenty-four hours of fever. Only a pediatrician or ER doctor can adequately diagnose this type of seizure.

Treatment

- Keep area safe.
- Do not try to restrain your child. Once started, the seizure will run its course no matter what you do. Try not to hold the child too close to you as that can increase the child's body heat.
- Once the seizure is over and your child is awake, give the usual dose of medicine (Tylenol).

WHEN TO SEEK MEDICAL CARE

- First febrile seizure
- Lasts longer than five minutes
- Neck stiffness
- Confused or delirious
- Difficulty awakening
- Any seizure activity in absence of a fever

Common Colds

It is quite common for babies less than 6 months old to have nasal congestion, provided there is no cough or rectal temperature over 101.5 degrees. Amazingly, we even have a term for it—the common cold. Babies who are in day care, church nursery, or play group can expect to have between four to eight viral colds between October and February!

Signs

- Runny nose
- Nasal congestion
- Possible fever, generally under 101.5 rectally
- Sore throat (usually determined by decrease in appetite)
- Cough with no difficulty breathing
- Watery eyes

Relief Measures if Approved by Your Pediatrician

- Use saline nose drops. Instill two or three drops in each nostril. Wait a few seconds, then use the bulb syringe to suck the saline out of the nostrils. Depress bulb, hold one nostril closed, and insert tip in open nostril. At the same time, slowly remove the bulb syringe while releasing the suction of the bulb and doing a sweeping motion in nostril. The first two days, you may use three to four times per day, then decrease to two or three times per day. Use preferably before meals and before bed. (See DVD.)
- The temperature in the home should be 68 to 70 degrees in winter, 72 to 74 degrees in summer.
- Dress the baby as you would dress yourself, as far as layering and seasonal appropriateness. If you are wearing long pants and a long-sleeve shirt, then the baby should be wearing the same. You may use a short-sleeve onesie underneath.
- You may use a cool mist humidifier.
- Elevate the head of the bed. Do not place any objects in the child's bed or crib. You may prop one end of a thick baby crib mattress up by placing a rolled-up regular-size towel underneath one end of the mattress. Do not exceed a 20 degree angle.
- If the nose is very runny and the baby is not resting well, check with your pediatrician.
- You may clean the outer lids of the baby's eyes with a warm washcloth several times a day.

Note:

Colds are not curable. Comfort measures are used to help with symptoms. No medicine approved in children will make the cold go away any faster. There are hundreds of different cold viruses, and most healthy children will get six to ten colds a year. Careful and frequent hand washing can help manage the transmission of these viruses. We recommend keeping baby wipes in several rooms of the house and washing down everyone's hands several times a day.

• If the baby has a fever, see the fever section of this book.

• Increase fluids. Children with colds may not want to eat, as they often swallow a bunch of mucus down the back of their throat. This makes them lose their appetite (understandably!).

WHEN TO SEEK MEDICAL CARE

• Frequent (several times an hour) cough with no improvement after doing above

• Chest sinking in when breathing

• Ribs pronounced during inhalations

• Nostrils flaring

• Wheezing (whistle or squeaking sound)

• Stridor noise made on inhale when not coughing; tight sounding

• Breathing faster than sixty respirations a minute

• Temperature is over 103.5 in a baby more than 6 months old; over 101.5 in a baby 3 to 6 months old; or at 100.4 in a baby less than 3 months old

• Symptoms last longer than ten days

• Pulling on ears and/or not sleeping well for two or three nights

• Worsening sore throat or copious (abundant) drooling

Falls and Lacerations

Be careful. We get about three calls a week from parents who left their baby on the bed, couch, or changing table for "just a minute" and then found them crying on the floor. This usually happens around 4 to 6 months old when the baby suddenly learns to roll over. Now, the good news is that God knew that babies would do this, and he specifically designed them to tolerate minor falls. Their bones are spongier than our brittle adult bones, and the three "plates" that will eventually form the skull (between 15 and 18 months) will allow for some minor swelling—unlike our adult "hardheaded" variety. The fall is generally much harder on the parent than on the baby; in other words, it scares the parent more.

Many falls, in our experience, result in a bump on the forehead. Usually the swelling can cause a "goose egg." There is not much soft tissue on the forehead, so it always looks big when swelling occurs. We would not notice the swelling as much on the leg because the soft tissue covers a good deal of it.

Head Injury with No Lacerations

- Do not give any pain medications. If pain is severe (i.e., half an hour of inconsolable crying), call your pediatrician.
- After your baby goes to sleep the first time after a head injury, make sure he or she can be awakened every thirty minutes for two hours. Keep in mind what is normal for your child.
- Check pupils (the small black area in the center of the eye) to make sure they get smaller when the child is exposed to bright light. You can take the baby into the bathroom and turn the lights off for one minute. Then turn the lights on and watch the pupils to make sure that they both get smaller in reaction to the lights coming on.
- If the fall was from a distance greater than four feet, you suspect that the neck got twisted, and/or if the baby is not moving or crying, *do not move the baby.* Immediately call 911.

WHEN TO SEEK MEDICAL CARE

Watch for these symptoms for forty-eight hours:

- Persistent vomiting (more than twice)
- Pupils not reacting to light by getting smaller, or one pupil is large and the other small

- Marked sensitivity to light

- Difficulty awakening; seems confused

- Breathing abnormally

- Extreme moods: either an hour of inconsolable crying or marked lethargy

- Not urinating

- Not moving a limb or sensitive when a limb is moved or touched

- Abdominal pain—the baby cries out when you touch the abdomen (make sure your hands are not too cold)

Lacerations

Clean the affected area well with soap and water. Apply pressure with a wet and preferably sterile 4 x 4 gauze pad for as long as it takes to stop the bleeding.

WHEN TO SEEK MEDICAL CARE

- If wound edges are not touching or wound is gaping

- Bleeding does not stop with pressure in five to ten minutes

- Bleeding is severe and/or pulsating out of the body

- Any laceration on the face

Note:
You have a right to ask for a plastic surgeon to repair any facial lacerations if you so choose. However, the best way to access a plastic surgeon is through the local ER.

Otitis Media (Ear Infections)

CALL "I'm not sure if my 5-month-old has an ear infection or is teething."

Ear infections usually start with a cold. The fluid that the cold produces becomes trapped behind the eardrum. Bacteria love to live in that warm, moist environment and begin to grow. Once the area has become infected with bacteria, babies generally experience discomfort.

Signs

- Ear pain (pulling at ear frequently)
- Crying when lying flat
- Not sleeping well
- Fever for more than two or three days (although ear infections are frequently present without a fever)
- Cold symptoms

Note:
Ear infections can occur in babies who have no symptoms at all. Sometimes we find ear infections in children who are being seen simply for a physical exam. These infections are an impossible problem to treat based on symptoms alone. The key is to watch your child for changes in the activities of daily living or for the classic symptoms described on this page. In the absence of symptoms, there is no way to know when to take your child to the pediatrician. However, if your child is only pulling at the ear but is sleeping and eating well, then it is okay to wait a day or two before making an appointment.

Treatment

- You may use OTC cold medicines only with your pediatrician's approval for babies over 14 pounds.

WHEN TO SEEK MEDICAL CARE

- There is no improvement of the above symptoms after treating with pain-control medicines.

- General rule of thumb for ear infections: if your baby has an interruption of two or more of their daily activities (sleeping, eating, and playing), see the pediatrician. For example, if the baby is (1) not sleeping well and (2) fussy all day, or if the baby is (1) not eating and (2) not sleeping, it is time to call the pediatrician.

Vomiting

CALL (from a dad) "My kid just threw up and I don't know what to do."

If your baby is less than 3 months old and is vomiting persistently, contact your pediatrician. Vomiting occurs when the baby forcefully and persistently empties his or her stomach every thirty minutes to one hour, regardless of feedings. Although there are various causes of vomiting, we see it most often associated with a gastrointestinal virus. These types of viruses usually start with vomiting every thirty to forty-five minutes for the first six to eight hours, then maybe an isolated episode of vomiting on day two or three. Diarrhea will often accompany these symptoms, and the diarrhea generally lasts for five to seven days (see p. 71).

Treatment

- Wait one hour from the last time your child vomited. Begin with one teaspoon of water or Pedialyte every ten to fifteen minutes, while the baby is awake, for three hours. After your baby has tolerated this for three hours, begin to increase the amount by adding a teaspoon every ten minutes for another three hours. (Sucking on a wet washcloth or giving fluids in a medication dropper at first are ways of ensuring that the child is not swallowing too much at once.)

- After six to eight hours, you may try to breast-feed a limited amount, increasing as tolerated, or use one to two oz. of formula every thirty minutes for two hours. Babies who are old enough to eat baby food can eat rice cereal or mashed potatoes in very small amounts. If the baby tolerates any of these items, you can feed several bites of these foods every fifteen to twenty minutes.
- If no vomiting occurs after twelve hours, begin returning to a normal diet slowly.
- If the baby vomits during any of above, return to the first step.
- If you're breast-feeding and the baby vomits twice, continue to breast-feed, but nurse on one side for ten minutes every one or two hours. If the baby vomits three or more times, wait one hour, then nurse four or five minutes every thirty minutes. If the baby goes eight hours without vomiting, return to the regular schedule.
- Avoid giving medicines for eight hours (with the approval of the pediatrician). If the baby is running a fever of 102 or higher rectally, use Fever-All suppositories if permitted by your pediatrician. (If the baby is less than 3 months old, a fever of 100.4 or higher rectally is considered an emergency.)

Common Errors

- Giving too much fluid at one time
- Not waiting an hour before beginning fluids

Sometimes when a gastrointestinal virus is causing vomiting in a child, no matter what or how often you feed him or her, the vomiting will continue. If your child is crying for fluids and it has not been an hour after vomiting, it is okay to give liquid; just try to have him or her drink slowly. (We realize that you have only so much control over how quickly a child drinks.) When a child is experiencing these symptoms, it is crucial to monitor for the following additional symptoms.

WHEN TO SEEK MEDICAL CARE

- Not urinating at least every six hours. (You may want to leave toilet paper in the diaper to check for wetness because the absorbent nature of diapers makes it hard to tell if the baby has urinated at all.)

- When you run your pinky finger over the inside of the baby's bottom lip, it is dry and tacky as opposed to smooth and moist

- Tries to cry but cannot cry tears

- Marked lethargy

- Unable to hold down one tablespoon of fluid after two or three attempts. (Remember to wait thirty to sixty minutes after each vomiting episode.)

- Vomits blood

- Neck stiffness

- Rash

- Vomiting that continues longer than twenty-four hours

- Fever

Note:
If the baby continues to spit up with every feeding, contact your pediatrician. See the chapter on spitting up (p. 93) for more information.

• Vomiting bile (fluorescent yellow or green goo)

• Vomiting that is severe and happening with every feeding in a baby less than 3 months old

• Abdomen hard and tender to the touch (hard like a tabletop as opposed to soft like a really full balloon)

• Blood in stool (more than one teaspoon of bright red blood)

• Baby is less than 3 months old and has a rectal temperature of 100.4 or higher or is more than 3 months and has a rectal temperature over 101.5

Spitting Up

Some babies spit up more than others. It is more related to physics than behavior. Spitting up usually resolves by 7 months, although babies may have a resurgence of spitting up when they learn to sit up because there is more pressure on the abdomen as those muscles are developed. The babies start to develop these great tummy muscles around 4 to 6 months old, while Mom is still trying to figure out how to stand up straight and is looking for a good girdle for her own tummy!

• Burp infant two or three times during a feeding. Do this when the baby pauses in a feed. If there is not a pause, then try every five to ten minutes.

• Place infant in a 35 to 45 degree angle (reclining position) for twenty to thirty minutes after the feeding. A bouncy seat is great for this.

Diarrhea

CALL "My 6-month-old has had diarrhea that exploded out of the diaper five times today. I've had to change his clothes every time."

Diarrhea can be caused by a gastrointestinal virus and can generally last five to seven days. However, sometimes babies may have a day of diarrhea secondary to mild stomach irritation, and this will pass in one or two days.

Signs

- The baby has more than five watery stools in a twenty-four-hour period

Relief Measures

We do not like to give medication that claims to stop diarrhea for children less than 2 years old because most diarrhea is caused by a gastrointestinal virus that will run its course. We want the diarrhea to get out of the baby's

Note:
Regardless of how you feed the baby, diarrhea will generally run its course. However, it's probably not the time to get Mexican for dinner if you are breast-feeding.

Note:
Diarrhea is very contagious. All family members need to wash hands well after changing diapers or using the toilet.

system. This is the body's natural way of handling this kind of virus.

- Formula-fed: You may switch to Isomil DF for a few days.
- Breast-fed: Continue to breast-feed. Breast milk is the gentlest thing for an infant's tummy.
- Give baby food for babies more than 6 months old. Starchy foods are good choices (i.e., cereal, applesauce, bananas, carrots, mashed potatoes).

WHEN TO SEEK MEDICAL CARE

- Eight or more watery stools a day for five days
- Watery stools in any amount for a baby less than 1 month old or a baby with poor weight gain
- Blood or mucus in stool
- Fever (ask your pediatrician for a fever handout)
- Abdominal tenderness and hardness at rest
- Any signs of dehydration:

  Longer than six hours without urinating

  No tears when crying

  Inside of bottom lip feels dry when you swipe your pinky finger across it

  Increased lethargy

71

Reactive Airway Disease/ Bronchitis/Bronchiolitis

CALL "I have been giving my baby the inhaler as directed, but the cough is more frequent and he is bringing up more mucus when he coughs."

Babies 4 to 6 months old can get upper respiratory infections, although it is more common in 6- to 24-month-olds. If your baby's doctor diagnoses any of the above diseases, you must monitor breathing very closely. Upper respiratory viruses can trigger the airways to swell and become narrower. These airways are lined with mucus, and when they narrow, it is hard for the child to dislodge the mucus. The medication Albuterol/Xopenex/Proventil will help open up the airway so the child can breathe better and dislodge the mucus.

What to Expect

In the first twenty-four hours of treatment, the child

- will get a more frequent, more productive-sounding cough. The cough will improve slowly after the first twenty-four to forty-eight hours and should be markedly improved within five days of beginning treatment.
- may seem to have a rapid heartbeat and may be on the hyper side for the first night or two of treatment. This is the trade-off for being able to breathe and will subside in a day or two.
- may have isolated (i.e., not persistent) episodes of vomiting (mucus triggers the gag reflex).

WHEN TO SEEK MEDICAL CARE

Sometimes the airways do not respond to the medications in a way that improves breathing. Here are some of the signs that the symptoms are getting worse.

- The ribs get more pronounced when inhaling (retraction). You can almost count the ribs with each inhalation. This is an indication that the child is using accessory muscles to move the air in and out of the lungs. The child is working too hard to get the air he or she needs.

- Respirations are faster than sixty times in one full minute. Put your hand on the child's chest and count how many times the chest rises in one minute. If you count more than sixty, recheck in three to four minutes; if still above sixty, seek medical care. Normally, a baby or young child will breathe twenty to thirty times per minute.

- Bluish or purplish hue around lips

- Shortness of breath with moderate activity

- Audible wheezing (a squeaky sound when exhaling as opposed to a rumbling or mucusy sound)

- Coughing so frequently that the child cannot get air in between coughing fits

- Mucusy-sounding breathing that is not cleared with a cough

- Symptoms are unchanged after the first twenty-four hours of treatment

Infant Nasal Congestion

CALL "I have a 3-week-old infant with a stuffy nose. I think she caught my cold."

It can be normal for infants to have nasal congestion, provided there is no cough or rectal temperature of 100.4 degrees or higher. We even have a term for it—infant nasal congestion.

Relief Measures if Approved by Your Pediatrician

- Use saline nose drops. Instill two or three drops in each nostril. Wait a few seconds, then use the bulb syringe to suck the saline out of the nostrils. Depress bulb, hold one nostril closed, and insert tip in open nostril. At the same time, slowly remove the bulb syringe while releasing the suction of the bulb and doing a sweeping motion in nostril. The first two days, you may use three to four times per day, then decrease to two or three times per day. Use preferably before meals and before bed. (See DVD.)

- The temperature in the home should be 68 to 70 degrees in winter, 72 to 74 degrees in summer.
- Dress the baby as you would dress yourself, as far as layering and seasonal appropriateness. If you are wearing long pants and a long-sleeve shirt, then the baby should be wearing the same. You may use a short-sleeve onesie underneath.
- You may use a cool mist humidifier.
- Elevate the head of the bed. Do not place any objects in the child's bed or crib. You may prop one end of a thick baby crib mattress up by placing a rolled-up regular-size towel underneath one end of the mattress. Do not exceed a 20 degree angle.

WHEN TO SEEK MEDICAL CARE

- Frequent (several times an hour) cough with no improvement after doing above

- Chest sinking in when breathing

- Ribs pronounced during inhalations

- Nostrils flaring

- Wheezing (whistle or squeaking sound)

- Stridor noise made on inhale when not coughing; tight sounding

- Breathing faster than sixty respirations a minute

- Temperature is over 103.5 in a baby more than 6 months old; over 101.5 in a baby 3 to 6 months old; or at 100.4 in a baby less than 3 months old

ROUTINE ISSUES

*Feeding Information
and How to Get Your Baby
to Sleep through the Night*

- Eat 2½ to 3 hrs
- 30 mins to eat
- ⊙ 3 options:

1/ Nursing only. 1 breast = meal
2 breast = dessert

2/ Nursing/topping off

1 breast
1 bottle (formula/b/milk

(2/3 Weeks) 3/ Bottle

9pm Feeding

Start 3oz.
Bottle dry? ↑ ½oz - 1 oz

$$\frac{Formula}{2/3 \ Weeks?}$$

Pump
Start to pump 2/3 weeks. Late night.

Breast-Feeding

CALL "I am worried that my baby is not getting enough milk."

Many breast-feeding moms share this concern. We cannot measure, in ounces, how much breast milk a baby swallows each feeding. However, we do have some guidelines that are helpful in determining if the baby is getting the breast milk he or she needs.

Knowing the Baby Is Getting Enough

- The baby is nursing at least eight times in twenty-four hours. You may drop down to six or seven times around 4 to 8 weeks old. Longer stretches at night are acceptable.
- The baby is satisfied after nursing.
- The baby urinates at least every other feeding or at least every six hours.
- The baby gains approximately half an ounce a day for the first few weeks (with the exception of the first week, when newborns commonly lose weight).
- The inside of the bottom lip is smooth and moist.

- The soft spot is not markedly sunken.
- Periods of alertness last at least twenty to thirty minutes several times a day.
- The letdown reflex is present for the mother.

How Often and How Long?

- The first one or two weeks, nurse on demand. Thereafter, every two and a half to three hours is sufficient during the day. At night, you may go longer, as much as five to nine hours if the baby was full term and is at least 2 weeks old, healthy, and beginning to gain weight.
- After your milk comes in, usually by the eighth day at the latest, feed as long as your infant wants (up to twenty minutes) on the first breast. That ensures your infant is getting the high-fat, calorie-rich hind milk. You can tell the baby has finished when the sucking slows down and your breast is soft and mushy. Then offer the second breast if the baby is interested. Remember to alternate which breast you start with at each feeding.

Latching

- For the rooting reflex, bring the baby close to your breast, then stroke the baby's cheek. Your baby's head will turn and mouth will open.
- Put as much of the areola into the baby's mouth as possible. Never allow the baby to suck on the nipple only. This will hurt you and not provide as much breast milk as the baby needs.

- Holding the breast from below will help put it into the correct position.
- Place the baby's body directly facing the breast.
- If the baby is not latched on correctly, remove the baby's mouth by placing a finger gently in the corner of the baby's mouth to break suction. Try the above steps again.

Positions

- **Cradle hold.** Sit the baby in your lap with the baby's head in the crook of your arm. The baby's chest should be against your chest so that the baby does not have to turn his or her head to reach your nipple. Remember to give him or her a little room to breathe through the nose.
- **Lying down.** Lie on your side and place the baby on his or her side facing you, with the baby's head at your breast.
- **Football hold.** Hold your baby like a football along your forearm, with the baby's body on your arm and his or her face toward your breast. Use your other hand to support the position of the baby's head.

Find a relaxed and comfortable position. Change positions with different feedings. Use pillows for your back. Boppy pillows or other nursing pillows are great. These saved my (Jennifer) aching back when I was nursing my twins.

Breast Care

Nipples

- After each feeding, coat nipples with some breast milk.
- Allow nipples to air dry.
- If nipples are cracked, apply 100 percent lanolin to them after feedings. (If allergic to wool, do not use lanolin.)
- Make sure the infant is latching correctly.
- If you're sore, begin feeding on the less sore nipple.
- If the pain is severe, you may need to pump until nipples heal.

Plugged Ducts

These are hard, tender lumps in your breast, caused by incomplete emptying of the breast milk.

- Nurse on the tender side first.
- Massage the breast with the lump, trying to express extra milk.
- Apply moist heat to breast. Take a hot shower while massaging and expressing extra milk. Do not let the shower be so hot that you feel faint.

Engorgement

You may have large, firm, and tender breasts that will last until your body gets used to making and releasing milk. Once your baby is nursing well and the milk is flowing easily, there will be less swelling and firmness.

- Warm breasts with a warm washcloth before nursing.
- Gently massage breasts while nursing.
- Apply a cool washcloth to breasts between feedings.
- Put crisp, cold, green cabbage leaves thoroughly washed and dried over your engorged breasts. Leave on for twenty to thirty minutes until leaves are wilted.
- If engorgement makes it difficult for the baby to latch on, you may need to pump or hand-express some milk before feeding.

Mastitis (Breast Infection)

These symptoms include aches, flulike feelings, a fever, chills, headache, breast pain or redness, firmness, nipples that sting or burn, shooting pains in your breast during nursing, and painful lumps.

- Call your ob-gyn immediately if you have any of these symptoms.
- Take the entire antibiotic prescribed.
- Rest and stay in bed (as much as is practical with a newborn).
- Drink plenty of fluids.
- Nurse more often, especially on the side that is infected.
- Apply a warm washcloth to breast before feeding.

Storage and Handling of Breast Milk

- Wash hands well.
- Store milk in plastic rather than glass.

- Label each bottle with the date and time expressed.
- The bottle may be stored in the refrigerator for seventy-two hours; stored in the freezer (5–15 degrees Fahrenheit) up to three months; or stored in the deep freezer (0 degrees and below) up to six months. It may be stored in the refrigerator for twenty-four hours after thawing.

Thawing

- Thaw under running warm water or in a bowl of warm water. Make sure the nipple stays above the water line at all times. I (Laura) like to microwave a standard coffee mug filled halfway with water. When I take the mug out of the microwave, I put the bottle of milk in it so the hot water surrounds the outside of the bottle and warms it. The two-ounce plastic bottles often fit nicely into a mug.
- Do not thaw milk at room temperature. Bacteria can grow in it.
- Do not allow thawed milk to sit for more than two hours at room temperature.
- Do not refreeze thawed milk.

Amounts

- Allow twenty to thirty minutes to eat. Taking an hour to feed a healthy infant is too long. See the lactation consultant.
- Begin with two ounces at a time. Add more until the thirty-minute mark. For example, if the baby finishes three ounces for two feedings in a row, then have three

and a half to four ounces in the bottle for subsequent feedings. This ensures that the baby can eat more if he or she is hungry.

- Never reuse breast milk that is left over in a bottle after one hour.

Vitamins and Supplements

Consult your physician at the two-month checkup to guide you in vitamin supplementation.

Herbs and homeopathic remedies are usually not tested on infants and children less than 6 years old. Therefore, we cannot recommend any herbal preparation. That is not to say that they are harmful. There is just not enough information available about their safety when used in children or infants.

Gas in Breast-Fed Infants

- Empty one breast completely before switching breasts.
- Burp well and often.
- You may use infant gas drops according to package label. These drops break big air bubbles up into little air bubbles so they are easier to pass. Use before feedings or after feedings.
- Infants make more gas than adults do. It is okay to leave gas untreated.
- Babies get fussy in the evenings. They often draw up their legs and make strange faces. This does not necessarily mean that they are in pain. Again, think of what you would have to do in order to pass gas while lying down.

85

Formula-Feeding

CALL "I started my baby on Lipil, and then he was fussy, so I changed him to Isomil. He was still fussy, so the next day I tried Carnation Good Start."

One important factor when deciding to change to a new formula is that it takes a baby's digestive system five to seven days to adjust to the new enzymes and sugars in a new formula. Do not switch unless advised by the pediatrician, and then expect five to seven days of fussiness, gassiness, and changes in bowel habits.

Note:
Formula companies are regulated, and formulas are designed to meet the nutritional needs of your infant.

Store-brand formulas from Wal-Mart, Target, etc., are available. Some brand names of formulas include

- Ross products (Similac, Similac Advanced, Isomil, etc.);
- Mead-Johnson Products (Enfamil, Enfamil Lipil, Prosobee, etc.).

Types of Formulas

Powder

- Least expensive
- Can be prepared ahead of time
- You may use a blender with short pulses, then allow the mixture to sit in the refrigerator for a few hours before serving. Do not serve right away or it's gas city!
- Use warm tap water to mix formula and store in the refrigerator for up to forty-eight hours. Using tap water ensures the baby is getting some fluoride. In some places, boiling tap water is necessary. If you are using well water, boil it for five minutes and let it cool.

Concentrated

- Equal amounts of tap water and formula
- Can be stored in the refrigerator for up to forty-eight hours

Ready-to-Feed

- Most expensive
- Does not contain any fluoride

How Often and How Long?

- Newborns will usually eat two to three ounces every three hours, or six to eight feedings per day, for the first 3 weeks; five to six feedings per day from 1 to 3 months; and four to five feedings per day from 3 to 7 months. Then they drop to three to four feedings per day from 7 to 9 months.

- A feeding should not take longer than thirty minutes. If it is taking longer than thirty minutes after the baby is more than 2 weeks old, contact the pediatrician.
- The amount of formula can vary from feeding to feeding and day to day. Some days they need more and some less, just like us. Between twenty-four and thirty-two ounces of formula a day is generally sufficient for healthy babies.
- Never reuse formula left in a bottle for over an hour.

Amounts

- Begin with two ounces at a time. Add more until the thirty-minute mark. For example, if the baby finishes three ounces for two feedings in a row, then have three and a half to four ounces in the bottle for subsequent feedings. The baby does not have to finish it all; simply have more to offer.

Position

Make sure that both you and your infant are comfortable.

- Support your arm with a pillow or use the crook of your arm.
- Hold the baby in a semiupright position.

- Tilt the bottle so that the nipple and the neck of the bottle are always filled with formula.

Changing Formulas

- Do not change formulas without checking with the pediatrician.
- If formula is changed, it will take the infant several days to adjust to a new one.
- Stools will change, may increase or decrease, and can vary from firm to loose.
- The baby will have increased gassiness and fussiness.

Temperature for Feedings

You may try different temperatures from cool to warm to find which your infant prefers. If warming, place bottle in a cup of warm water and *always* check temperature before feeding.

Gas in Formula-Fed Infants

- You may try different bottle systems. Gerber with the flesh colored, old-fashioned-looking nipple is our favorite and the least expensive. More expensive does not necessarily mean better quality, just better advertising.
- You may try different nipple sizes.
- Burp well; try different positions when burping.

• You may use infant gas drops according to package directions.

When a baby has occasional spitting up, it bothers us as mothers more than it does the baby. Try to take your cues from how well the infant tolerates the spitting up.

There is a condition called GI reflux that can be treated with medication. If your baby is very fussy throughout the day and during feedings, contact your pediatrician.

Note:
Never reuse leftover formula from a bottle. The bottle must be finished or the unused portion discarded after one hour. Once the baby's mouth has touched the bottle, bacteria has been introduced into the entire bottle. Refrigeration does not kill the bacteria.

Spitting Up

CALL "My doctor prescribed some reflux medicine for my baby, but he still spits up three or four times a day. Will this ever end?"

Occasionally babies will vomit or spit up after a feeding. When to be concerned:

- Persistent vomiting (i.e., every thirty to forty-five minutes) regardless of feedings
- Vomiting large amounts at least two or three times a day for more than two days
- Forceful vomiting more than six times a day
- Vomiting progressively getting worse with each feeding
- Baby's stomach clenches within minutes after feeding begins
- Unable to keep latched on
- Fussy with feedings, during and after (although this alone can also indicate a growth spurt)
- Decreased wet diapers. We like to see at least five wet diapers in twenty-four hours. Check diaper well. You

may want to place toilet paper in the diaper to check for wetness.

- Inside of bottom lip is dry and tacky when you swipe it with your pinky finger
- Abdomen hard and tender at rest
- Blood in stool (more than one teaspoon of bright red blood)
- Baby less than 3 months old has a rectal temperature of 100.4 degrees or higher
- Baby 3 to 6 months old has a rectal temperature over 101.5

Note:
If the baby continues to spit up with every feeding, contact your pediatrician.

Some babies spit up more than others. It is more related to physics than behavior. Spitting up usually resolves by 7 months, although babies may have a resurgence of spitting up when they learn to sit up because there is more pressure on the abdomen as those muscles are developed.

- Burp infant two or three times during a feeding. Do this when the baby pauses in a feed. If there is not a pause, then try every five to ten minutes.
- Place infant in a 35 to 45 degree angle (reclining position) for twenty to thirty minutes after the feeding. A bouncy seat is great for this.

Starting Baby Foods and Solids

CALL "When can I start baby foods? I need to know how much to feed my baby and how often to feed her."

You may begin baby food (stage one) between 4 to 6 months of age. The babies need to be

- sitting with support;
- holding their head up well;
- appearing hungry after feedings;
- able to hold their head up and push up on one elbow when they lay on their tummy. (That's a strength thing. We don't feed them on their tummies!)

Begin with baby rice cereal. Mix one or two tablespoons of cereal with formula or breast milk until the consistency is like yogurt. Use the long-handled spoons and place the food on the tip of the spoon. Place the spoon in the baby's mouth and allow it to sit in the baby's mouth while you hold it. The baby may spit the food out, and it can be very messy. Be patient; it sometimes takes an infant ten to fifteen times of trying a new food before he or she likes it or can even swallow most of it. Be prepared to wear a good deal of baby food over the next month. (See recommendation for Biz laundry soap in the general shopping list on p. 21.)

Do not use mixed cereals (i.e., barley and oat mixed together) until you have tried the cereals individually for at least three days in a row. Remember, at this stage amounts are not important. The baby may take one or two spoons one day and five to six the next. Your baby is getting all his or her nutritional needs met through the formula and/or breast milk up to one year of age.

Starting Baby Food Fruits and Veggies

- Start baby vegetables and fruit after the baby is doing well on rice cereal for about a week.
- Try one new baby food at a time.
- Always start new foods in the morning to see if it agrees with your baby.
- If the new food seems to upset the baby (increases fussiness and spitting up), stop that food and wait one to two weeks to try it again.
- Begin with a one- to two-ounce jar, then increase it every day or two by one ounce as tolerated by the baby. You will know the baby is full when you are wearing more food than the baby is eating and he or she is increasingly distracted.
- Do not feed the baby out of the baby food jar; pour the food into another container and feed from there. The bacteria from the baby's mouth (by way of the spoon) will contaminate the jar of food. Once opened,

an uncontaminated jar should be refrigerated and used within forty-eight hours.

- Remember, amounts are relative at this stage.
- You can mix one type of baby food with the baby cereal three times a day for three days before adding a new food. Then you can add another food to the overall diet. For example, after mixing the apples with the rice cereal every feeding for three days, mix bananas with rice cereal in the morning and then apples with rice cereal in the afternoon for three days. Then you can have apples/rice in the morning, bananas/rice in the afternoon, and peas/rice for dinner for three days!

Sippy Cups

You may begin putting small amounts of water or formula in a sippy cup around 6 months of age. The baby may sip only occasionally, and it will take time for him or her to learn how to suck out of this type of cup.

- Place the tip of the sippy cup on the tongue and hold it there for a few minutes if well tolerated.
- Make sure that the baby is not choking on milk that is leaking from the lid.
- You may offer the sippy cup frequently, even if your baby only wants to play with it at first.

Food Allergies

Do not give peanuts or peanut butter until after 2 years old.

Common Reactions

If you notice the following symptoms, use Benadryl and avoid suspect food for at least two weeks.

- Splotchy pink areas on face only (no facial swelling)
- Diarrhea and/or vomiting
- Itchy skin areas, exacerbates eczema
- Gassy/fussy

Less Common Reactions

If you notice the following symptoms, use Benadryl and avoid suspect food for at least two weeks.

- Sore throat or frequent throat clearing
- Nasal congestion, runny nose, sneezing, sniffling

Severe Reactions

If you notice the following symptoms, call 911!

- Sudden difficulty breathing and/or swallowing
- Wheezing
- Tightness in chest or throat
- Excessive drooling
- Facial swelling
- Hivelike splotchy rash all over (together with any of the above symptoms)

You may need to see an allergist if food allergies are suspected.

Getting Your Baby to Sleep

CALL "My baby is 3 months old. She cries every night and wakes up two to four times to feed. I am so exhausted I can hardly think straight."

Now here is the real reason most of you will be reading and loving this book! If you follow these directions, you will have a much better chance of enjoying your evenings and nights now and on into toddlerhood.

After evaluating that there are no physical abnormalities in the baby, the following advice—if followed—will produce a much better night's sleep.

Note:
In order to begin the Moms on Call method of getting your baby to sleep, the baby must be at least 2 weeks old, healthy, and gaining weight.

The Basic Moms on Call Sleep Principles

- Keep at least three hours between the "supper" and "bedtime" feedings so the baby is hungry for that last feeding, which will have to carry the baby through the night
- Do not allow any naps after 6:00 p.m. to last longer than 1½ hours and all other naps should not last longer

97

than two hours. Many babies think that nighttime starts at 6:00 p.m. with a few hours of fussy awake time between 7:00 and 9:00 p.m. We want to allow them to have a good nap in the morning and early afternoon and sleep all night.

- Correctly swaddling a baby less than 3 months works wonders (see p. 105). Think of it as recreating your tender embrace.
- We do not recommend swaddling a baby more than 3 or 4 months old, as he or she is usually strong enough by then to wriggle out.
- White noise must be loud enough for you to hear it clearly from the other side of a closed door.
- Routine, routine, routine. Babies will associate bath time, swaddle, darkness, and white noise with bedtime.
- Once the baby goes in the bedroom for the night, he or she stays in the bedroom. Prepare the bottle in the kitchen while the baby is still in the bed, even if the baby is crying. Do not bring the baby to the living room to watch TV while you feed at night. You do not want to have any additional stimulation such as bright lights or TV noise at night. Nighttime is the time for sleep and time to be in the bedroom. Keep the middle-of-the-night feeding as boring, dark, and quiet as possible—in the baby's room.

Naptimes

- Put the baby in an area where there is light and moderate noise.

98

- Swaddle tightly (babies less than 3 months old).
- Put the child in the crib or bed while awake.
- You may use white noise. We recommend purchasing a sound-soothing machine with no lights. They can be found at Target, Wal-Mart, and the Sharper Image. You can also play a CD of white noise on a boom box. Homedics makes the SS-200 Sound Spa, which we like a great deal.
- Naps should last no longer than two hours at one time. Until 4 months of age, a late evening nap up to an hour and a half in length is fine. From 4 to 6 months of age, there should be no naps after 6:00 p.m. that last longer than an hour.

2½ hrs
Nap
till 4wks
After
4wks
2hrs

Bedtime
Bath
Swaddle

Bedtime Routines

Begin with bath time. After the baby is bathed, diapered, and clothed, dim the lights, read a book, and play soft music (see DVD). Our (Jennifer) family loves Bible stories for bedtime reading. I will also hold the kids and tell them that they are brave and strong and how proud I am of who they are. It is never too early to begin to speak blessings over your children!

- Feed very well. Burp.
- If the baby is between 2 weeks and 3 months old, swaddle tightly using the Moms on Call swaddle blanket.
- Place the baby in the bed on his or her back.
- Turn on white noise.

Goal

Dont feed before I am

- Make sure the room is dark. Avoid night-lights or closet lights. You may turn on minimal lighting when you go into the room to check on the baby so you do not trip.
- Let the baby cry it out starting with five to ten minutes of full-on crying. The timer starts over if he calms down. For a baby less than 4 weeks old, allow five minutes maximum of continuous crying, then try repositioning the baby. If needed, allow five more minutes of crying and then try a pacifier, five more minutes and then try reswaddling, and so on. Gradually add a minute or two as the baby gets older.

Meet Goal

Move Goal to 15-30 mins

Babies *will* fall asleep. If you are consistent, after three days they will sleep at bedtime in the crib and fall asleep almost immediately—but only if you do not go in their room to pick them up at every little noise or mild period of fussiness. Give it three nights. You can do it!

every 3-5 nights

Middle-of-the-Night Feedings

Healthy babies more than 2 months old will not starve because they miss a feeding at 2:00 a.m.! We can teach them how to sleep through the night and drink what they need during the day. They will be more content on the fourth day than they have been in months—and so will you, if you let them learn to sleep at night and eat during the day . . . just as adults do.

Feed on demand until the baby is 2 weeks old and gaining weight, then you may start these interventions.

- Always wait until the baby is truly crying—not fussing and just making noises, but full-on crying.

100

- Try to wait five minutes in the beginning to make sure the baby does not go back to sleep. Set the clock.
- Feed with the least amount of light that is safe and as little talking as possible.

Note:
Once they are rolling over and scooting around in the bed, take the swaddling blanket out of the bed.

- Keep it boring. This feeding is strictly business.

If you would like your baby to sleep for eight to ten hours in a row, follow these instructions to the letter. And remember to follow these steps for at least three nights in a row before you decide for certain if they work. No cheating!

Getting your baby to sleep is really easy if you are convinced that the best thing you can do for him is teach him how to soothe himself to sleep. Resist the overbearing need to hold him any time he cries. I (Jennifer) had to fight the urge to hold my first son all day and night!

We often sit outside the door torturing ourselves for those three nights, listening to the baby crying and feeling like a failure. We become afraid that our baby will suffer abandonment issues, among many other things. Let's set the record straight: our babies will suffer if they never learn to sleep through the night and they never learn how to soothe themselves to sleep! They need a solid routine, and they need us to let them cry it out in a safe environment for three nights.

Note:
Sleeping with a baby less than 6 months old can be quite dangerous. There is a great risk that you could roll over on the baby when you are in the deepest of sleep and cut off the baby's air supply. We do not recommend cosleeping.

You can check on the baby every five to twenty minutes, but try not to pick him or her up. Use the paci-

101

fier, rub the baby's tummy, or reswaddle if needed. If the crying persists, you can feed the baby (see p. 116). We know that this is hard, and we have shed our own tears as we listened to our kids cry it out, but guess what? Every one of our eight kids sleeps through the night, as do kids in thousands of families who use this method. But before you start, you have to be absolutely com-

Note:
The temperature in the room should be between 68 and 74 degrees so the baby does not get overheated while crying.

mitted. (Usually dads are more committed than moms, so let Dad encourage you, and enjoy night four and every subsequent night thereafter!)

The sound-soothing machines that are available at Target or Wal-Mart are an essential piece of the puzzle. Be sure to get one intended for adults so they do not have all those annoying lights. They need to be loud enough for you to hear them clearly from outside the baby's room with the door closed.

Something that works just as well is a baby monitor unplugged from the base so the static is loud enough for you to hear through the door.

Use this routine, and do not leave out one step! This has worked for thousands of frustrated families, and it is our hope that it will be just as effective for you and yours.

The Amazing Swaddle

CALL "I cannot seem to swaddle my baby like the nurses did at the hospital. She keeps wriggling out of it in five minutes. Is there some sort of trick to this?"

Yes! There are many things that we have discovered about the swaddle. In order to achieve a tight, effective swaddle, the blanket has to be large and square. The blankets sold at popular retail stores are too small. That is why we developed and manufacture (trust us, this was not easy for two working moms with eight children!) our own 44 x 44-inch large flannel wonders. The second thing that you need to achieve a tight swaddle is an effective technique with a demonstration. We developed the DVD so parents could watch the demonstration several times over, see how the swaddle is done, and know how tight to make it.

The primary benefit of the tight swaddle is to reduce the baby's startle reflex and imitate the snug environment of the womb. Healthy babies are born with a startle reflex. This is an involuntary reaction to the movement in the arms that they cannot control. Many parents will say, "He likes to have his hands up by his face, so I do not swaddle the arms." However, babies less than 2 months old do not have purposeful movement of their limbs. They cannot

103

keep their hands up by their face in the same way that they cannot hold their own bottle. If a baby's hands are up by her face, they will move, startle the baby, and wake her up. Swaddling her with her arms by her sides prevents the startle reflex and helps her sleep better. Think of it as a reminder of your tender embrace.

Babies may not seem to like the swaddle at first, but they just need the opportunity to get used to it. Once they do, they will begin to associate swaddle with sleep and sometimes drift off before you can finish tucking in the last piece of material.

It is important to mention that babies can get overheated. The temperature in the room should be between 68 and 74 degrees when the baby is swaddled to avoid overheating.

Swaddle Tips

- The ideal time to start the nighttime routine is after the baby is 2 weeks old and is gaining weight.
- We do not recommend swaddling a baby more than 3 to 4 months old.
- Watch the DVD several times and swaddle and re-swaddle until you feel like you have it right.
- Before you put the baby on top of the blanket, spread the swaddling blanket on a large, adult-size bed, where it is easiest to perform the swaddle. Fold over the first corner. The corner's tip should be almost touching an imaginary line between the adjacent corners.
- Remember to pull the slack out of the blanket with each fold.

104

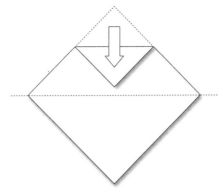

- Begin making the "pocket" when you fold the last corner over the baby's chest and around the back.

- The last corner that tucks into the "pocket" should be slightly wadded and not completely flat. This will help the swaddle to remain secure.

- When you wrap the final corner around the baby—the "belt"—it should be level with the baby's elbows not shoulders.

- Do not use fabric softener when you wash your Moms on Call blanket; it may smell good but will be too soft to keep secure.

Note:
The Moms on Call swaddling blankets are available online at www .momsoncall .com. They are generally delivered within two business days.

These guidelines should help you produce the tight hospital swaddle that makes babies feel secure and sleep better. If you follow the above instructions and the baby is routinely able to wriggle out of the swaddle, then it is time to change to a zip-up sleeper and take all swaddling blankets and sleep positioners out of the bed so they do not become a danger.

Crying

CALL "My baby cries, and I cannot stand it!"

Infants Less Than 1 Year Old

Healthy babies may cry on and off for three to four hours a day, more often in the evenings.

- If the baby cries for two hours *nonstop* (does not have five- to ten-minute periods of not crying), he or she needs to see the pediatrician.
- Occasionally check fingers, toes, and penis (if applicable) for hair or thread wrapped around these areas. You need to look closely. If unable to remove hair, call your pediatrician.
- Also check eyes for redness or excessive watering when not crying. Occasionally a baby may scratch an eye with a fingernail.

106

Common Causes of Crying in Infants

Milk Allergies

* Severe crying, usually after every feeding
* Vomiting
* Watery stools or stools with less than one teaspoon bright red blood for more than three stools (do not have to be consecutive)

Note:
Always see your pediatrician to check for any medical problems with continuous crying and/or vomiting.

Acid Reflux

* Spitting up after every feeding, often painful high-pitched crying immediately thereafter
* Forceful vomiting more than three times per day for more than two days
* Crying with meals, day and night
* Arching back
* Unable to keep latched on breast/bottle

Comfort Measures

* Swaddle tightly. Remember, if the swaddle is not tight, the baby will not like it. Some babies will act like they do not like it until it is done. The advantage of using a tight swaddle is that it keeps babies from startling themselves. Babies have not yet figured out how to control their limbs. This is very irritating if one is trying to get to sleep! You may stop swaddling at 3 to 4 months.

- Tilt babies toward their bellies either on your forearm or across your lap.
- Turn on white noise, which needs to be louder than the crying.
- Be in constant motion, always supporting the head and neck.
- After your baby has calmed down, try to give a pacifier. (Teach them to suck a pacifier by pulling on the pacifier while they are sucking and allowing them to pull it back in with the suction of their mouth.)

Overstimulation

- A baby 0 to 6 months old cannot handle the hustle and bustle of the adult lifestyle. Make sure that all the naps are not in the car "on the run."
- Be aware of your child's limitations.
- Allow time for quiet play.

The Three-Day Rule

CALL "We are at my mom's for vacation and Sterling does not want to sleep. She usually goes to sleep so well. She has just been fussy ever since we got here."

This baby will probably take three days to adjust to her sleep schedule once the family returns from vacation. This happens in our lives very often.

Take heart: the three-day rule will ring true. Hang in there and keep that bedtime routine as consistent as possible. Knowing what to expect and living in that reality will greatly improve your ability to cope.

We have found that babies and toddlers require a three-day transition period in many areas. Do not get discouraged. Continue to provide a routine environment. Children's sleep patterns may be interrupted when

- they reach certain developmental milestones (i.e., crawling, walking, speaking);
- they change environments or daily routines (vacations, holidays);
- they are recovering from an illness.

This is where the sleep cycle can meet its doom. It is hard to retrain babies to go to sleep on their own and stay in bed after all these interruptions. If you stay committed, they will learn in about three days. That is how long it takes babies to establish a new routine or reestablish an old one. So they will fuss and cry like they did when you were training them to go to sleep the first time. It gets better with each subsequent night.

When I (Laura) moved my 2-year-old, Brent, into his new room, he did not want to take a nap. I put him in the childproofed room, closed the door, and allowed him to cry. The first day took about twenty minutes of crying (which seemed like forever at the time!), the second about ten minutes. By the third naptime he fussed for only about two or three minutes and was off to sleep. Did this break my heart? Yes. Was this the best thing for Brent so he could learn to soothe himself to sleep? Definitely.

Now, let's look at a different scenario. If I (Laura) had allowed Brent to come out of the room, he would have had this crying episode at every nap in order to be able to do something more fun. He also would have been incredibly tired and cranky for the rest of the night, which would be particularly unfortunate since I have four other children to manage. If I had given in and stayed with Brent until he fell asleep, I would have taught him how to be dependent on my presence in order to fall asleep. This would also affect nighttime sleeping. Say good-bye to date night, alone time, and any needs arising from the other four kids, since Brent requires a mommy or daddy to get to sleep. Can you see where we're going with this? Teaching our children to get to sleep on their own will benefit the whole family, and it is truly the right thing to do for our kids.

Frustration

Babies cry. It is okay to allow your baby to cry fifteen to twenty minutes at a time. She may cry on and off for three to four hours, especially in the evening. We do not want your baby to have more than two hours of inconsolable crying, and we are not asking you to ignore her basic needs such as diaper changes and feedings. Just be prepared for babies to cry for no apparent reason in the evenings and for fifteen- to twenty-minute segments during the day. It does not necessarily mean you are doing something wrong.

Children learn by practicing. They do the same thing over and over again. It may take thirty times of doing something the wrong way—or even the right way—before they consistently do it the right way. Continue to allow them the opportunity to learn.

If your child is about to crawl and is crying for a toy across the room, do not get it for her. Her frustration level can motivate her to achieve developmental milestones.

Allow the baby a moderate level of frustration and crying. Monitor and encourage her as she tries to crawl, walk, and soothe herself to sleep.

Typical Days

Most babies thrive on a routine. However, the times below are a guideline and can be adjusted to your schedule. Remember, try to keep as close to you and your child's daily routine as possible.

We understand that schedules these days need to be flexible. We know that the babies who have regular naptimes and feeding times tend to be more content. There is a delicate balance between being so scheduled that you cannot enjoy life and being so flexible that you cannot enjoy your baby.

Babies can be very fussy on the first night home from the hospital. Most of the time, babies are sleepy during the day and fussy at night. Babies can be difficult to awaken for feedings during the day. At night they may seem as if they want to feed every hour. They will adjust their schedules in a week or two. It is important that you try to sleep when the baby sleeps and recognize that this stage does not last forever. For the first four weeks, schedules are being established, and they may vary considerably from day to day. Some babies are on a schedule from the start and eat every three hours, day or night. You will know what kind of baby you have.

Set Marker

2 to 8 Weeks

- 6 a.m.—Feed
- 7 a.m.—Sleep
- 9 a.m.—Feed (baby is generally alert and playful with mild, if any, fussiness)
- 10 a.m.—Sleep
- 12 p.m.—Feed (baby is generally alert and playful with mild, if any, fussiness)
- 1 p.m.—Sleep
- 3 p.m.—Feed (baby is generally alert and playful with mild, if any, fussiness)
- 4 p.m.—Sleep
- 6 p.m.—"Supper" feeding (baby is generally alert and playful with increased fussiness as the night progresses)
- 7 p.m.—Baby may sleep up until bath time (may have increasing fussiness)
- 8:30 p.m.—Begin bath time routine. Stretch this time out so baby is hungry for the last feed of the night.
- 9–9:30 p.m.—"Bedtime" feeding (can start as early as 9 p.m.)
- 9:30–10 p.m.—Baby may be put down as early as 9:30 p.m. but no later than 10:00 p.m. Swaddle very well, put in bed, turn on white noise, and make sure the room is dark. Allow the baby to cry. (You may let the baby cry for five to ten minutes if less than 2 months old. Try increasing that time as the baby gets older.)

- ♪ a.m.—If awake (truly awake—do not count whining, grunting, or straining), wait just a few minutes prior to feeding. Try pacifier.
- ♪:15 a.m.—Feed (keep it boring)

Allow babies to sleep as late as they want to within reason. Adjust as needed for your schedule. Usually babies should start their day by 9 a.m.

Another scenario is to feed "supper" closer to 7 p.m., start bath time at 9:30 to 10 p.m., and give the "bedtime" feeding around 10 to 10:30 p.m. This is great to begin with for a couple of weeks.

The most important thing is to always keep a minimum of three hours between the supper and bedtime feedings. The bedtime feeding should always come after the bath.

8 to 16 Weeks

Babies can transition to this schedule anytime between 8 and 16 weeks of age when they are regularly sleeping from 9:30 p.m. to 7a.m.

- 7 a.m.—Feed (baby may sleep or remain awake and playful)
- 8:30 a.m.—Nap (ideally for one to one and a half hours)
- 10:30 a.m.—Feed
- 12 p.m.—Nap
- 2 p.m.—Feed (baby is generally alert and playful with mild, if any, fussiness)
- 3 p.m.—Nap

- 4:30–5:30 p.m.—"Supper" feeding (baby is generally alert and playful with fussiness increased from the morning)
- 6 p.m.—Catnap
- 7 p.m.—Wake up, stimulate, play (this time on and off fussiness may be moderate to severe)
- 7:30 p.m.—Begin bath time routine.
- 8 p.m.—Begin bedtime feeding and routine. When sleeping from 10 p.m. to 6 a.m. consistently, you may begin to start the bath time/bedtime routine earlier.

When starting the bath time/bedtime routine earlier, some feedings combine. Some feedings may need to be two and a half hours apart and others closer to four hours apart. Remember to keep in mind that the "supper" and "bedtime" feedings are the only ones that need to be a minimum of three hours apart.

The amount of milk your body produces generally depletes as the day goes on. That often makes breast-fed babies a little fussier with evening feedings. It is fine to supplement at those feedings.

You will begin to take the baby out of the swaddle around 3 to 4 months of age (earlier if the baby is wriggling out on his or her own).

Remember, for every change that occurs in the baby's routine, allow *three days* to adjust.

4 to 6 Months

- 7 a.m.—Wake up; give formula/breast milk

- 8 a.m.—Cereal with half a jar of fruit (you may begin to give sippy cup of water or milk)
- 9 a.m.—Nap (one to one and a half hours)
- 10:30–11 a.m.—Formula/breast milk (introducing a sippy cup here is fine)

Note:
Our goal is to give the baby at least twenty-four oz. a day or three to four good breast-feedings.

- 11:30 a.m.–12:00 p.m.—Two to four oz. veggies; two to four oz. fruit (remember, this is a gradual progression)
- 12:30–1:30 p.m.—Nap
- 2:30–3 p.m.—Formula/breast milk
- 4 p.m.—Two to four oz. veggies; two to four oz. fruit, plus a sippy cup of formula/breast milk. If the baby has not fed well or has not taken the sippy cup well, pour remaining formula/breast milk into a bottle and let the baby finish the rest from the bottle.
- 5 p.m.—May take a catnap
- 6 p.m.—Keep awake from now until bath time/ bedtime
- 7 p.m.—Bath time routine
- 7:30 p.m.—Breast-feed or bottle feed
- 8 p.m.—Bedtime routine

SAFETY ISSUES

Ways to Keep Your Baby Safe

Immunizations

CALL "Can I give my baby Tylenol before his immunizations to help it not hurt so much?"

Tylenol will not take away the pain of the actual injection. As a matter of fact, the baby will have forgotten the incident by the time you walk out the door. (It will probably take *you* much longer to forget.) We all get through it. We hate it, but we do get through it.

Site of Injection

- Given in thighs or arms
- May be red and/or swollen for two or three days at site of injections
- May have small, pea-sized knots for several weeks after discoloration resolves

Fever

- A fever of 101 to 103.5 rectally is expected for up to forty-eight hours after the immunizations are given

119

(with the exception of the 12-month immunizations). Because immunizations are started when the baby is 2 months old, the forty-eight hours after the 2-month immunizations is the only time that a fever 100.4 or higher is tolerated. Your pediatrician should send home a handout about common side effects of immunizations and when to call.

- Tylenol may be given every four hours. See package instructions.

WHEN TO SEEK MEDICAL CARE

- Temp over 103.5 rectally

- Crying inconsolably for two hours

- Seizure activity (uncontrollable shaking)

- Signs of allergic reaction (very rare) within the first fifteen to twenty minutes after administration of immunizations

    Difficulty breathing

    Wheezing

    Hives

    Paleness and clamminess

    Difficulty swallowing

Vaccinations

Moms on Call is in favor of vaccinating children. It is what the American Academy of Pediatrics recommends. Although the MMR (measles-mumps-rubella) vaccine is not administered until 1 year of age, you may have heard about studies linking the MMR vaccine with autism. There are studies that disprove this theory as well. However, that is the nature of studies—it takes several years and millions of dollars to make any definite connections. This much we do know: prior to the MMR vaccination, more than 100,000 children a year died of these combined diseases. If your child does not get immunized and contracts one of these diseases, it puts him or her and other children at risk, especially children less than 1 year who have not yet been vaccinated.

The types of vaccinations that your child will get at 2, 4, and 6 months generally include

- DTP (diphtheria, tetanus, pertussis);
- IPV (injectable polio vaccine);
- Prevnar—protects against bacteria that can cause meningitis and pneumonia;
- HIB (*Haemophilus influenzae* type B)—another bacteria that can cause meningitis;
- Hep B (Hepatitis B)—a disease of the liver transmitted through the blood and body fluids of infected carriers.

Note: In the summertime, especially when the baby's legs are exposed, the baby may try to pull off the Band-Aid and eat it. Watch carefully!

Some of these immunizations are combined in one shot, so the most your child should get at one time is four shots: two in one thigh, two in the other. It is over very quickly.

After immunizations the baby is generally a little sleepier for three to four hours, then possibly fussy for the next four to six. You can take the Band-Aids off after about an hour. If the baby is fussy or develops a fever, use Tylenol every four hours as needed.

At 9 months your baby may get a tuberculosis skin test. This is not an immunization against tuberculosis; it is a test to see if your baby has ever been exposed to it. The nurse will inject a small amount of tuberculosis antigen under your baby's skin on the forearm. This is generally harmless. Three days later, you look at the forearm and determine if the area that had the skin test is red *and* swollen. If it's just red but not raised, that is considered a negative result, which means your baby has not been exposed to tuberculosis. If you notice any raised quality or swelling at the site of the skin test, contact your pediatrician. The doctor will most likely ask you to come in so he or she can measure the area of swelling and then send your baby for a chest X-ray to determine if any tuberculosis has settled in the lungs. If the X-ray is normal, your doctor may put your baby on a regimen of antibiotics to help prevent any symptoms from occurring. These TB skin tests are routinely performed every year or two.

Childproofing and Safety

Real situation: *A 3-year-old choked on a carrot at home and the mom did not know what to do. Luckily the urgent care was minutes from her house, so she drove him there and the nurses dislodged the carrot before he became unresponsive. Close call? Yes. Did this mom want to take CPR classes after that? Yes!*

Accidents are just that—accidents. However, there are measures that we can take, such as childproofing and being knowledgeable about possible hazards, to help minimize risks for our children.

We find that parents spend much more time worrying about the relatively low risk of possible meningitis and less time worrying about the most common risk—injuries.

We cannot stress enough the importance of taking regular CPR training. The question you should ask yourself and your child's caretakers is not only, "When did I take my last CPR class?" but more importantly, "If my child were choking or unresponsive, would I know what to do?" (Yes, I know you said "call 911" in your head, but there are life-saving steps you can take while 911 is on the way!)

Please, please, please—know what to do if your child is choking. CPR classes are offered through the American Heart Association and the Red Cross. Almost all area hospitals offer regular classes.

Common Safety Tips

Here is a quick but not exhaustive checklist for some common safety issues.

- Put plastic guards on all sharp corners.
- Put outlet protectors in outlets not being used and outlet cover attachments on outlets that *are* being used. Children will try to play with cords that are plugged in.
- Keep any cords for blinds short and out of reach of children. Do not place the crib next to a window with cords hanging down.
- Put safety latches on all cabinets and drawers.
- Move all cleaning supplies from under the sink and put in a high cabinet that locks.
- Put plastic doorknob covers on doors and a hook-and-eye latch on any doors leading to basements or stairs.
- Keep a set of keys to all doors in case your child locks himself or herself in a room.
- Keep all plastic bags out of reach, including dry cleaner bags and grocery bags.

COMING SOON TO
MADEWELL.COM
OUR SISTER STORE'S EXCLUSIVE COLLABORATION
WITH STYLE ICON ALEXA CHUNG.
SIGN UP FOR THE SCOOP
AT MADEWELL.COM.

Madewell

SINCE 1937

ALEXA CHUNG

FOR MADEWELL

- Install infant gates at top and bottom of stairs. Use hardware-mounted gates, not pressure-mounted ones.
- Never allow children to play with latex balloons. They generally like to bite them, and they can inhale a piece of latex and choke or suffocate. No balloons in the car.
- Check the safety of the crib. Slats should be no wider than two and three-eighths inches apart. There should be no more than two inches between the mattress edges and the crib.
- Do not put pillows, stuffed animals, or anything else in the bed. If you think your child needs more warmth, use a sleeper (fleece zip-up). Swaddling blankets can be used until the baby is consistently breaking out of the swaddle, which is generally around 3 months old. Foam bed positioners should be taken out of the bed as well when the baby is able to wriggle out of them.
- Do not use pillowlike bumper pads in the crib.

Bathroom

- Keep all medicines in a locked cabinet and out of the baby's reach. This means no bottles of vitamins or Advil on the counter, even with "childproof" caps.
- Keep shampoo and soap out of reach.
- Always unplug any appliances to avoid electric shock.
- Set hot water heater to 120 degrees Fahrenheit. Always check temperature of water before placing child in it.

- Be aware of what you put in the trash (i.e., pills or razor blades). These items should be put in a trash can out of the child's reach.
- Put toilet locks on all toilets. I know Dad does not like this, but children are fascinated with the toilet and can fall in. They also like to flush items down the toilet, and Dad will not like taking apart the toilet to extract the large clump of Play-Doh. (Thanks, Patrick and Blake.)
- Always drain water out of the bathtub immediately after using it.
- Put nonskid bath mats on the bottom of the tub.
- *Never leave your child unattended in the bathtub!* If the phone rings, let it ring! The caller can leave a message.

Kitchen

- Always turn pot and pan handles to the back of the stove and cook on back burners.
- Avoid tablecloths. They can be pulled down, causing hot food to fall on the baby's head. When I (Laura) was a child, I pulled on a tablecloth, and a pot of hot grits fell on my foot. The burn marks are still there.
- Keep all appliances out of reach.
- Place covers on stove knobs and a lock on the refrigerator. (They sell these in all colors so they match your kitchen decor.)
- Always be aware of where your child is when transporting hot foods or liquids.

126

- House rule: No toys on the kitchen floor. You can trip and drop hot liquid on kids.
- Keep aluminum foil and plastic wrap out of reach.
- Make sure the stove is anchored to the wall. Make sure all knives and cutlery are out of reach. Sometimes latches on a drawer are not quite enough.
- Never keep kid snack food near any medications, vitamins, or cleaners. Kids learn which cabinet the snack food is in and try to get into it when you're not looking.

Living Area

- Be aware of windows on the second level or above. These should have safety locks so they can be opened only a few inches. Locks may be purchased at home improvement stores.
- Check all furniture to see if it falls over easily, especially bookcases. Where we see a bookcase, a little boy sees a ladder. Trust me (Jennifer), Bryce loved to try this. Anchor your bookcases to the wall.
- Keep electrical cords out of reach. TV cords can be pulled and cause the TV to come crashing down on a child's head.
- Never leave your child alone with pets.
- Always check stair railings for sturdiness.

Choking

- If the child is coughing vigorously and can talk and breathe, then do nothing. Do not slap a choking child on the back when he or she is in the upright position. This can lodge the foreign object in the throat.
- Removal of a foreign object is best learned in a CPR class.
- Do not put your fingers in the child's mouth unless you see an object. Only then can you perform a finger sweep of the mouth.
- Liquid that is swallowed at meals will usually clear itself in ten to thirty seconds.

Car Seats

- It is best to have your car seat checked by a professional. The website www.nhtsa.dot.gov will list area checkpoints. (Click on "Vehicles & Equipment," then "Child Seats," then Child Passenger Safety Training Contacts by State.") Some local fire departments will also check your installation; call first to see which location near you does so. This requires an appointment.
- Your car seat will come with weight limits. Check the side and back for information on placement and weight requirements.
- Infants should be rear-facing and in the second row of vehicle seats until they are both one year old and weigh twenty pounds.

- Straps need to be snug. The front clip should be at the nipple line, and no more than two of your fingers should fit between the strap and your child. Again, note the manufacturer's guidelines. If you have any questions, visit a checkpoint near you.
- When tightening the seat in the car, put your knee in the base of the car seat. Then thread the seat belt through the car seat according to the manufacturer's guidelines. The seat should move no more than half an inch from side to side. Always remember to use the additional safety clip (often sold separately) to clip to the seat belt. The safest place to put a car seat is in the middle of the back seat. Never put a child less than 12 years old in the front seat of a car with an airbag. The airbag can deploy with such force that it instantly kills a child.
- Never put the car seat in the front seat of a car.
- Many newer-model cars come with a tether attachment in the rear of the vehicle. Tether equipment can also be purchased at most baby stores.

Quick-Grab First Aid Kit

You will need the items below when you least expect to. Keep one kit in the car and one at home. These items are to be kept out of reach of children. We recommend buying a container with a handle and a lid. On the inside of the lid, list the pediatrician's number, the Poison Control number, and the "in case of emergency" phone numbers.

- Band-Aids
- Children's Tylenol
- Benadryl
- BD digital thermometer
- Cortaid
- Polysporin
- Antibacterial wash
- Hydrogen peroxide or Betadine
- Pack of 4 x 4 gauze and 2 x 2 gauze
- Ace bandage
- Squeezable ice pack
- Tweezers
- Dressing tape

Poisoning

CALL "I just gave my child a dose of Tylenol, and I didn't know that my husband had already given her some."

Poison Control: 1-800-222-1222 (toll free)
Local Poison Control (fill in)_____

Always call your poison control center immediately if you think your child has swallowed a poison or other substance, such as medicine, that he or she shouldn't have.

You will be asked the following:

- What was swallowed?
- How much? (Always estimate the maximum amount.)
- How long ago was it swallowed?
- What symptoms, if any, is the child showing now?
- What is the age and approximate weight of the child? Keep in mind that dads do not always get to go to visits to the pediatrician and may not know what the child weighs. Post the child's most recent weight on your refrigerator.

Prevention

- Keep all chemicals, medicines, and cleaners out of reach and locked.
- Get a list from a local nursery of any poisonous house or outdoor plants. For example, holly berries are poisonous. Get rid of all poisonous house plants.
- If someone in your household drinks alcoholic beverages, keep the beverages out of reach and locked.

THE LABYRINTH OF HEALTH CARE

How to Navigate through the
Health Care System

The Doctor's Office

People at Your Doctor's Office

Front-desk personnel. They cannot answer medical questions. They handle day-to-day operations such as locating your chart, making copies of records, and making appointments.

Billing and insurance. They are trained in billing. They do not answer medical questions. They may also be in charge of doing electronic referrals to specialists, which involves contacting your insurance to let them know why your child requires a specialist's care.

Office manager. This person is in charge of running the office. Generally, he or she is in charge of personnel. This person would handle complaints about office policies or poor customer service.

Staff nurses. These nurses generally call you and your child into the back office area and grill you with questions that the doctor will soon ask you again. There are many levels of nurses, and not all are trained to answer your medical questions. Here is our understanding of the educational background of the people who may be asking you questions, taking blood specimens, and giving immunizations.

- **Medical assistant.** Obtained a high school diploma and graduated from a six- to twelve-month medical program. Trained in basic medical procedures such as vital signs and drawing blood.
- **LPN (licensed practical nurse).** Obtained a high school diploma. Went through a one- to two-year program and took a national licensing exam. Trained in dispensing medication and basic medical procedures. Also trained in basic disease processes and administering medications and immunizations.
- **RN (registered nurse).** Obtained a high school diploma. Have at least a two-year college degree and completed a two-year nursing program. Took a national licensing exam. Trained in all the above plus in-depth disease processes, decision making, and patient monitoring.
- **BSN (bachelor of science in nursing).** Graduated from an accredited college of nursing that offered a four-year program. Trained in all the above plus administrative and ethical decision making.
- **Lab technician.** Obtained a high school diploma and graduated from a six- to twelve-month medical program. Trained in obtaining specimens of all sorts (including urine, blood, and feces), how to order tests, deciphering insurance information, and how to run a laboratory.

We have worked with people from all these specialties. There are some medical assistants and RNs who are wonderful and some who are not. It is always best to ask the doctor your questions during the office visit. Some advice is different because of the nature of the information. For example, not all doctors prefer the same brand of formula.

When calling your doctor's office for advice, the office should have trained phone triage personnel who can answer your questions. The doctors will seldom answer your questions over the phone themselves. In the offices where we have worked, we have more than 125 calls a day, and if the doctors had to answer them, there would be no time to see sick children. However, there are instances when the doctor likes to handle questions over the phone personally, and it would be a good idea to speak with your doctor about what those instances are.

Those Who Can Diagnose and Treat Your Child

Doctor. This person has graduated from an accredited college of medicine and took a national licensing exam.

Nurse practitioner. This is an RN who went back to school for a two- to four-year program that concentrated on diagnosis and treatment of disease processes. These practitioners are usually very patient-oriented, and if your child's case goes beyond their comfort level or educational expertise, they will call in the doctor to give a second opinion. However, in our experience, nurse practitioners are skilled, competent, and an excellent source of current information.

Physician's assistant. This person is not necessarily a nurse but must have a general knowledge of medical practices to be admitted to the PA school. PAs must also have a minimum of a high school diploma before being considered for the two-year program that concentrates on diagnosis and treatment of disease processes. PAs are generally more procedure-oriented and are trained to assist with minor surgical procedures.

Scheduling Appointments

If you ever had to wait for your appointment with a screaming child after a night of no sleep, you have probably been frustrated by this difficult health care system.

- **Main schedule.** This is a master schedule that has been set in place in advance by the doctors. It dictates when and how many appointments will be available each day. For example, there might be six physical exam slots—three in the morning and three in the afternoon. Sick visits may be every fifteen minutes in between.
- **Working schedule.** This includes changes that are made to the main schedule to accommodate everyday challenges. For example, during the middle of flu season, more sick visits need to be added to accommodate all the sick patients.

It is virtually impossible for the office to schedule the exact time each visit will take, even if each parent is screened before an appointment is made. "My child just has an ear infection; it will only take a second" can turn into a diagnosis of reactive airway disease that requires two breathing treatments, complicated take-home medicines, and a thorough explanation. We have seen this happen many times.

138

Here are some tips to help your doctor's office stay on schedule.

- **Be clear about what you want to have addressed at the visit.**
- **If you think you may want other siblings seen, say so when you are scheduling the appointment.** This is a prime cause of scheduling delays. Once you are in the room, try not to ask the doctor if he or she can see a sibling. If it turns out that you do not want another child seen, it is much easier to cancel that appointment than it is to stop everything, find the chart, make the right paperwork, and fit another child in front of existing appointments. On occasion, you simply do not realize that another child is sick until after you are put in the back office. Just try to evaluate both children prior to your visit if you can.
- **Arrive on time.** Why do you have to be on time when it often takes twenty to thirty minutes to get you to the back office? Well, it is essential that your doctor's office has a good idea of which patients are coming and at what time. Occasionally they have to "fit in" a child who is very sick. Some appointments are scheduled at times directly before lunch or closing time. It can require five or six employees to facilitate your visit from check-in to checkout. In the winter season, doctors and nurses rarely get more than a twenty-minute break all day.

One Saturday, the office we work with was open from 8:30 to 11:00 a.m. At 11:30, as the staff was getting ready to leave, a mom walked through the door with her son in his soccer uniform and demanded to be seen. "What is the problem today?" the front-desk person asked. "I think he has strep throat," the mother replied. As it turns out, the mom had taken this child to a soccer game knowing he had a fever and sore throat, therefore exposing both teams to what turned out to be strep throat. This is not a mistake anyone wants to repeat, and this mom was really not looking forward to making that dreaded call to the coach.

If you think your child is sick, and definitely if he or she has a fever, make an appointment and come to the office. Our kids play sports, and we understand the disappointment they feel when they are unable to participate. However, we are sure the other moms at the game would appreciate your consideration.

- **Have your insurance card ready.** Yes, the insurance agencies require that your doctor's office verify that you showed proof of insurance for every visit. They can deny a claim and postpone or deny payment to your pediatrician's office if the office cannot provide proof that you showed current insurance coverage. Simply stating "nothing has changed" is, unfortunately, a thing of the past.

- **Be understanding.** There are times when children become critically ill very quickly, and health care workers have to address the most life-threatening situations first. On some days this could mean that there have to be "work-in" appointments for five or six very sick children. There is no way to plan for how many or how severe the complaints can be. One critically ill child can throw off a schedule by an hour or more. The thing to remember is that your child would receive the same treatment if he or she were in imminent danger.

- **If you think that you have been overlooked, alert the front office staff politely, and they can check into the wait.** Different doctors have different schedules. Doctor A may be running on time and Doctor B an hour behind. Sometimes the staff may ask if you want to see another practitioner. Sometimes there is nothing that can be done. Asking politely can alert the front office if the charts got out of order or misplaced.

Phone Triage

This is our specialty! With a large call volume, especially in the winter, it can take up to an hour or more to get a question answered. Here are some tips to help you make this a positive experience.

- **If possible, do not call with a general question on Monday morning.** If you can avoid calling on Mondays altogether, that would be even better. If you are calling about a general question such as feeding issues, it is best to wait until the slower periods—between 11 a.m. and 12 p.m. or after 2 p.m. on Tuesday through Friday.

- **Ask questions during the visit.** Make a list before your visit so you do not forget your questions in the hustle and bustle of the visit. If you have a physical scheduled, do not call two days in advance to ask general questions. The checkup is designed to address those concerns.

- **Ask general questions during office hours.** After-hours phone triage is designed to determine if your child needs to go to the ER or not. It is not the time to discuss bowel habits in detail. If you have medication questions or are wondering if your child needs immediate medical attention, call after hours. Diaper rash is not an after-hours emergency. Your pediatrician's office would rather have you call than be worried about your child on any account, but please be courteous and do not abuse this privilege. In the winter months especially, triage nurses are inundated with calls about very sick children. Call if you need to, but take time to consider if your call could wait to be handled during office hours.

- **During regular office hours, if you do not hear back from the office in one hour, call back.** If it is winter and the call volume is overwhelming, the front office will tell you. However, there are several reasons that triage nurses may be unable to reach you, such as numbers entered incorrectly, computer malfunction, or human error. They should not look at a call and say, "Oh, that's silly; I'm not calling *her* back."

  After hours, if you call and need to speak to the phone nurse, you should receive a call back. If you do not hear back in thirty minutes, call the number again and tell the answering service. Do this until you hear from your pediatrician's office. If you have an issue that cannot wait thirty minutes, you should head to the local ER.

- **Be available.** We know it is difficult and sometimes even impossible to stay put for an hour, but be clear as to what number you can be reached at for the next hour. Do not call at a time when you know you could be reached at two or three different numbers.

- **Do not expect antibiotics to be dispensed over the phone.** It is unsafe medical practice to prescribe antibiotic therapy over the phone, especially for a child who has not been examined. On several occasions, the "ear infection" that a mom was so sure of turned out to be meningitis or pneumonia.

  Taking antibiotics when your child does not need them can make the antibiotics ineffective when your child does need them. I'd rather come to the office every time I think my child has an ear infection than put his life at risk when he is hospitalized for pneumonia and his immune system does not respond to treatment. Your doctor's office does not ask you to come into the office just to irritate you or collect your copay.

- **Carefully read the information that the pediatrician's office sends home with you after a visit.** We get many calls about immunization side effects. These are addressed on several fliers that pediatricians send home after immunizations are given. It is a good idea to have a file or drawer where you store these items.

  Look through this information prior to calling. It can be overwhelming to leave a doctor's office after immunizations with a crying infant and then have the presence of mind to read six sheets of instructions. That is why we recommend having a special place for the papers, so you can refer to them if you have a question or concern. If the answer you are looking for is unclear or not included in the flier, then call.

Medical Insurance

In a nutshell, medical insurance is a service provided to a group of people who agree to pay a premium (set amount) every month. That money is invested and set aside to pay for medical treatments for the people in that specific group. Insurance works because many people pay and then do not need expensive medical treatments. However, just because you have insurance does not mean that all medical expenses are covered. Some insurance companies do not pay for mental health services, some do not cover physical or occupational therapy, and some do not cover certain drugs. If you are on an insurance plan, you probably have a textbook that outlines all of the treatments that are covered by your insurance policy. You may need a law degree to decipher what they all mean, but it is your responsibility to be aware of your insurance company rules and regulations.

The following are some common problems.

- **You are unsure of the copay amount.** The copay (amount you pay at time of service) should be listed on your card. If it is not, contact your insurance company and ask for a list of copays. Your copay for the doctor's office may be different than your copay for an ER visit.
- **You do not have a primary care doctor.** Your insurance company lists all the doctors you can see in that insur-

ance plan. Some even require that you choose one doctor to be your "primary care physician" (the one doctor, the gatekeeper, you always must see). He or she orders lab work and decides whether to refer you to other specialists. Generally all the doctors that practice in the same office are covered by your plan, but it is always wise to ask the billing person at the office to be sure.

- **You are unsure what drugs or laboratories are approved.** Some insurance companies pay only for certain drugs or allow your child's testing to be done only at certain laboratories. This list can change monthly. If your insurance has a website, print out a copy of current drugs and laboratories that are approved prior to your visit. This list will help your doctor and make for less time spent at the pharmacy.

- **You are unsure if there is a need for a referral.** Referral does not mean that the insurance company will pay for services; it is only a notification process. It generally takes two or three business days to have a referral approved. You can check on the status of a referral by calling the customer service number on your card. It is a good idea to do this at least two days prior to a visit to a specialist or before having a procedure at the hospital.

- **You do not know what insurance plan you carry.** There are HMO, PPO, POS, and many other insurance plans. Your specific type of plan is not always listed on the card. If you are uncertain about your plan, contact your insurance company today and find out what plan you are on. You can write that information on the back of your card as long as you do not obstruct any printed information. This information is essential.

Who's Who at the Hospital

If your child needs to go to the hospital, you will encounter many men and women dressed in scrubs and hospital wear who all look alike. Here's an idea of who they may be.

Doctors. They usually have their name embroidered on a white lab coat. Surgeons usually wear scrubs. They should introduce themselves upon entering your child's room. The doctor on call from your child's pediatric office will usually come to see your child the morning after admission. These doctors will usually come to your room between 6:00 and 9:00 a.m. or after 5:00 p.m. If you have questions for them at other times, you can ask your nurse.

Some hospitals have "admitting doctors" who work for the hospital and handle your child's care in place of your personal pediatrician. These doctors usually have special training to aid them in how to best handle your child's case. If you have a doctor like this, your personal pediatrician will generally not come to see your child in the hospital but will keep in close contact with your child's admitting doctor.

Staff nurses. They have "RN," "BSN," or "LPN" on their badge. They administer your child's medication and assess your child every shift. They are also the ones to answer your questions and organize your child's procedures.

Nursing assistants. They help take care of basic needs, such as changing bed linens and taking vital signs. They are not trained in disease processes and do not answer medical questions.

Physical therapists. They are trained in how to use movement to aid in the healing process. They organize an exercise and movement regimen that helps teach your child how to move. These are prevalent in orthopedic units.

Respiratory therapists. They are trained in how to assess lung function and breathing. They can give breathing treatments and arrange for oxygen if needed.

IV team. Some hospitals have a staff dedicated to starting and maintaining your child's IV. They do not know about your child's specific medical status.

Lab techs. They are trained in how to draw blood and collect body fluids for testing. They do not know about your child's specific medical status.

Educators. They help you understand treatments and train you for home care. They are often licensed nurses.

Lactation consultants. They are usually nurses with specialized training in the area of breast-feeding. They can often be accessed even after you leave the hospital by calling the hospital and asking for the "Lactation Department."

Food services. They deliver and pick up meals. It is easy to get meal plans wrong because they change frequently. Ask your nurse what your child's meal plan specifications are so you can know if your child has the right type of food (i.e., bland, low salt). If you know your child is diabetic, the little sheet of paper that comes on the food tray should say "low-sugar diet" or "diabetic diet." Do not assume the Jell-O is sugar free.

Housekeeping. They can come in at any time and change the trash bags or take care of spills.

Maintenance. They can fix the air-conditioner or equipment in the room. If your air-conditioner is not working properly, you may have to wait all day to get maintenance to arrive. Keep in mind that they are taking care of a large facility.

Nursing supervisors. You will probably never see these people. They manage staff complaints and arrange for appropriate staffing.

Billing. You are usually required to stop by the billing office after discharge to discuss your bill. In some cases payment is required. Payment plans are usually an option if you are unable to pay the full amount. If you have insurance, the hospital will generally bill you after the insurance has paid their portion.

Patient advocates. If you are experiencing any problems, from arranging for child care so you can stay with a sick sibling to financial concerns, the patient advocate can direct you to the right helper.

Chaplains. There are often several faiths represented in the chaplaincy of the local hospital. If you need someone to listen to you or pray with you for your child's care, chaplains are an amazing resource. Many hospitals also have a chapel, a quiet place that can be used to spend time in prayer. They will often have Sunday services that are generally "nonoffensive" in the message.

The Emergency Room

Emergency services at a hospital include all of the people mentioned in the previous chapter. However, the ER, or ED (Emergency Department), as some are now called, also acts like its own specialized area. It is important to note that the purpose of the ER is to get your child out of immediate danger.

The ER is not a place to diagnose or treat a long-term illness. The people there do not manage immunizations or basic child care. They are mainly there for life-or-death situations. Yes, they can diagnose the insidious ear infection or strep throat and prescribe antibiotics for such. However, their primary purpose is to evaluate your child and make sure that he or she is not in any immediate danger.

If your child is in danger, they manage the situation until the child is in a stable enough condition to either be sent home or be admitted to a room in the hospital. This is why the wait can be so long.

If your child is not in immediate danger, he or she may have to wait in order of urgency. That means the victim of a car accident, possible meningitis, or an asthma attack is admitted first.

There are many childhood illnesses that can be either life threatening or something that does not even require treatment. If you find yourself in the ER with a child who eventually gets sent home for monitoring and you are wondering why you ever went through all that waiting and worrying, remember that pediatrics is not an exact science in most cases. It is better to be safe than sorry.

General Procedure at the ER

1. **Check-in.** This is where you give your information, show your insurance card, and sign that you will pay for the services delivered. If your child is in immediate danger, yell for help when you enter the ER. Life-threatening emergencies are reason enough not to check in before treatment.
2. **Waiting for triage.** After you check in, you are sent to the waiting area. You will be called from this area to be examined and questioned by a nurse. Vital signs are taken and the nurse evaluates how urgently your child needs to be seen. This evaluation is relative to how sick the other patients in the ER appear.
3. **Waiting to go to an ER room.** After the triage nurse evaluates your child, you are sent back to the waiting room. In the winter, this step could take several hours.
4. **Called to the ER room.** A nurse will put you in a room and ask more questions. Sometimes an IV is started or vital signs are taken again.
5. **The doctor comes.** A doctor questions you again and then decides what testing should be done. The tests

are done in different parts of the hospital depending on what is ordered. Once an X-ray is ordered, it is put on the X-ray schedule, and someone from that department takes your child to do the X-ray. Lab work follows the same procedure. When the results come in, the doctor reviews them and either orders more tests or determines the problem and treats your child. Then you either go home or wait again for a room in the hospital to become available.

The ER manages emergency situations. Once you leave the ER, your child's care should be handled by your child's primary care physician. Sometimes children are released from the ER and then have another life-threatening episode. If this is the case, return to the ER. Your pediatrician generally will not come to see your child there; he or she leaves that assessment up to the discretion of the ER physicians.

Some hospitals have a staff of admitting doctors who follow your child's care even after your child has been admitted. These physicians will come daily to your child's room to perform evaluations and order tests and medicines. They keep in touch with your pediatrician by phone and fax. If you have this kind of doctor, your own pediatrician will not come to see your child in the hospital. The admitting physicians are often internal medicine doctors and are quite skilled at the types of things that cause children to be hospitalized.

The Specialist's Office

Your doctor has a general knowledge of a variety of medical conditions. However, specific treatment for a disease process or condition may require a doctor who specializes in that one area. If that is the case, your doctor will recommend that you make an appointment with a specialist.

In pediatrics, there are many specialties. It is best to have your primary care physician determine which specialist is needed. Many specialists' offices have long waiting times before an appointment is available. If your child's situation is urgent, your child's primary care physician can sometimes call and try to get your child in to see the specialist as soon as possible.

- Make sure the specialist is on your insurance. You can either call the customer service number on your card or look on the website to find out.
- Call your doctor's office and tell the referral coordinator the name of the specialist and the date and time of the appointment.
- Call your insurance company two days in advance of your appointment to check on the status of your

referral. You can ask whether or not it has been approved.

- Have your insurance card ready the day of the appointment.

If you do not take these steps, often you will have to wait at the specialist's office. Their staff will require time to call the insurance company and your doctor's office. This process can take up to an hour. I am sure none of us wants to wait with our child for an hour in any office!

If you do not need a referral, then off to the specialist you go.

Final Thoughts

It is our hope that these resources have given you confidence as you enter into that wonderful love affair called parenting. All babies have something unique and special to offer, and it is a privilege to watch their little personalities unfold. Each parent also has something special and unique to offer. No one can parent your child like you can.

If these materials have given you more time to enjoy smiles, giggles, and quiet cuddles, then we have definitely done our job. We know that you can be fantastic parents—not perfect, but realistic and ready for what lies ahead. Remember that we all make mistakes and learn from them. Use your helpers, ask questions, and don't forget to enjoy yourself. You can do this. We believe in you.

Don't forget to visit www.momsoncall.com for practical advice, information on parenting seminars, and those amazing swaddling blankets that calm, soothe, and help babies sleep! Because our business has been built on word of mouth, we ask that you tell your friends what a difference Moms on Call has made in your life. You can become one of the many testimonials that we post regularly on our website. Thank you for allowing us into your home, your heart, and your family.

Some Interesting Calls from Parents

"A chicken just fell on my child's head." *It was a frozen chicken and very heavy. The child was unharmed.*

"My child just ate six inches of dental floss."

"My child complained of his elbow hurting, so I rubbed turpentine on it. Is this okay?" *We do not recommend this!*

"I think my 10-month-old just said the word 'brochure.' Is that possible?"

"Our 2-month-old daughter is potty trained. We hold her over the potty twice a day, and she has her bowel movement in the toilet." *This is a first.*

"My child just bit the dog." *We get concerned when it is not the other way around, but it should be okay as long as the child did not draw blood.*

Phone conversation:
"What do you think this rash is?"
"I don't know. What do you think of this shirt I'm wearing? Do you like it?"
"I don't know. I can't see it."
"Exactly!"

156

"Is disobedience contagious?" *It can be.*

"I have an emergency. I am at the store and cannot find a Puffalump pet for my daughter." *Wow, should we come to help or send the ambulance?*

Phone conversation (2:00 a.m.):
"I am calling for my child's strep test result from last week."
"How is your child doing now?"
"Oh, she's sleeping and doing fine. I just wanted to know if the test ever turned out positive."
"That can be handled during regular office hours."

"I think my baby is fine, but my mom told me to dip my baby's pacifier in rum and then let her suck on it to calm her down." *We do not recommend this for the baby.*

Phone conversation:
(Dad) "My child has a fever of 103."
"Where did you put the thermometer?"
"Back on the shelf."
"No, I meant, 'Where did you put it in the child?'"

Phone conversation (2:30 a.m.):
"I need to know what to do if my child is constipated."
"How is the child now?"
"Oh, she's fine and asleep in her room. I was just lying here thinking that I'm not sure what to do if she ever got constipated."
"So she has not been having any problems with her bowel movements."
"No, not yet."
"Ma'am, it is two-thirty in the morning. With all due respect, if she ever actually gets constipated, call us."

Jennifer Walker, RN, BSN   Laura Hunter, LPN

Laura Hunter, LPN, is a mother of five, a pediatric nurse, an entrepreneur, and the most sought-after infant care consultant in the Atlanta, Georgia, area. The one common passion for all these areas of Laura's life is her desire to inspire and encourage parents.

Jennifer Walker, RN, BSN, is a mother of three, a pediatric nurse, a public speaker, and an author. Jennifer has over twelve years of pediatric nursing experience and has a heart to equip parents with practical advice and inspiration for the joys and challenges of parenthood. She lives and works in Atlanta, Georgia.

Visit the Moms on Call™ website at
www.**momsoncall**.com
to find more tips on getting your baby to sleep or to order
a special swaddling blanket for infants 0 to 3 months